SURVIVING SUBURBIA

Los Angeles Times
BOOKS

Editor: Carla Lazzareschi
Designer: Catherine Vandecasteele
Copy Editor: Betty Baboujon
Cover Illustration: Ethan Long

ISBN: 1-883792-69-X
Copyright 2003 Los Angeles Times
202 W. 1st St., Los Angeles, CA 90012

First printing April 2003
Printed in the U.S.A.

Los Angeles Times

Publisher: John P. Puerner
Editor: John S. Carroll
Book Development General Manager: Carla Lazzareschi

Peggy,
Very nice to
meet you. I hope
you enjoy the book.

Best,
Chris Erskine.

THE BEST OF "THE GUY CHRONICLES"

SURVIVING SUBURBIA

CHRIS ERSKINE

DEDICATION

TO CATHY AND THE KIDS

◆ ◆ ◆

◆ ◆ ◆

ACKNOWLEDGEMENTS

I'd like to thank Carla Lazzareschi, for editing this book and allowing it to happen. Thanks also to Betty Baboujon, one of the best copy editors in the business, and the other editors along the way who shepherded these columns through when they originally ran in the *Los Angeles Times*: Susan Freudenheim, Elena Howe, Nancy Yoshihara and Joan Springhetti. Thanks, too, to Catherine Vandecasteele, who designed the cover and the page you're reading now.

Special thanks to Michelle Williams, who had the sense of adventure to offer me a weekly column in the first place, and to Charlie Waters, an extraordinary editor and good friend.

Last, I'd like to thank the many folks, a dozen at least, who make the long walk to the end of the driveway every Wednesday, pick up the paper and turn to "The Guy Chronicles" as part of their morning routine.

◆ ◆ ◆

CONTENTS

◆ ◆ ◆

INTRODUCTION

My strong points are few and varied. I'm a good and grateful eater. I'm capable of long walks without rest, sometimes of a mile or more. And, when the mood hits me, I can be an extraordinary whistler.

Other than that, I am a pretty average guy with one great gift: an amazingly tolerant family who puts up with weekly revelations of a sometimes personal nature. Their good spirit and humor created this book. If you find it any sort of amusing, you have only them to thank. I'm just their typist.

"The Guy Chronicles" officially began in January 1998. This book is a collection of some of those columns and occasional essays that appeared in the *Los Angeles Times* before the column began. They are organized by the characters from the column and, as such, are not necessarily chronological.

They have in common a suburban setting, a leafy little place just outside Los Angeles. It's not middle America, but you may feel its rhythms. It's not Hollywood, but you can smell it from here.

Here's to our little town and the good people who call it home.

CHAPTER ONE

MY WIFE

♦ ♦ ♦

A Thousand Times Yes

ON the way to the movies, we argued about nudity, with me claiming that it just gets in the way of a good story and her insisting that it's OK as long as it is rampant and gratuitous, like on a honeymoon.

"You sure about nudity?" I asked my wife.

"Positive," she said.

Or maybe it was the other way around. Maybe I argued in favor of nudity. The point is, we were on a date.

Tired of discussing the Kennedys, we'd escaped to the multiplex on maybe our 1,000th date, each one better than the last, each one an adventure in marital romance.

"How about 'The Thomas Crown Affair'?" she asked.

"I love Steve McQueen," I said.

"This is the new one," she said.

"I love Faye Dunaway," I said.

We had come to see something else, then spotted "The Thomas Crown Affair" on the marquee, a special preview two weeks before it would open.

"I love Steve McQueen," I said again.

"This is a remake," my wife said with a sigh.

"I know," I said, "but I love the guy."

Steve McQueen. "Sand Pebbles." "Bullitt." Car chases and daring motorcycle rides. Talk about your guy movies. Sometimes there'd be kissing, but somehow they were still guy movies.

I'm flashing back to the original "Thomas Crown Affair," a cool romantic thriller from the late '60s, back when movie stars had chiseled cheekbones and icy eyes and they weren't afraid to use them.

Frankly, it's a short flashback, because I don't remember all that much about "Thomas Crown," except that it had McQueen as a millionaire thief and Dunaway as an insurance investigator, a woman of dubious morals, maybe fewer morals than a thief would have. Which can be an interesting trait in an insurance investigator.

In the end, I remember Dunaway waiting in a cemetery for McQueen to show up. A great ending. Almost all I remember is the ending, with the Rolls-Royce slowly pulling up and the jet streaking overhead.

"Let's go," I told my wife, and she nodded. A lot of nodding and impulsive decisions, both signs of a good date.

"Popcorn?" I asked.

"Sure," she said impulsively.

"Sno Caps?" I said.

"Why not?" she said with a nod.

As we waited in line for snacks, I bumped up against her shoulder, real softly, like on a first date. A gentle-gentle touch. Pre-foreplay.

"You have nice shoulders," I said.

"Quit bumping me," she said.

And we went into the theater, behind people who don't hold doors for other people, and we quickly discovered that all the seats in the middle were taken. One thousand dates and we've never had a seat in the middle.

It's as if these same people never leave, like they're always in the middle, living on movie food and mindless stimulation. The multiplex people, ruining it for everyone else.

"Over there," I said, pointing to a seat in right field.

"OK," she said.

So we sat down, sliding down low in the seats like teenagers do on their dates, looking almost straight up at the screen from our cheap seats there in right field.

"You sneak in some beer?" I asked her.

"I thought you were," she said.

And the previews started and it became impossible to talk. Used to be, it was rock concerts that ruined our hearing. Now it's movie trailers. Loud. Relentless. The Metallica of our middle age.

"Pass the popcorn!" I yelled.

"OK!" she yelled back.

Turns out, this remake of "Thomas Crown" is pretty good. The acting is so-so, but the new story is clever, with a terrific ending and some steamy romantic stuff that keeps the audience spellbound.

I know this because at one point the guy next to me was so spellbound that he stopped breathing. One moment, he was breathing really loud, through his mouth and ears, and the next he'd stopped breathing. Thought we were going to lose him, but when the movie ended, he got up and left.

"I liked it," I told my wife, gently bumping her shoulder as we left.

"I miss Steve McQueen," she said.

On the way home, we argued again about nudity, with me claiming that it just gets in the way of a good marriage and her insisting that it's OK with her, as long as it's rampant and gratuitous, like on a honeymoon.

Or maybe it was the other way around. The point is, we had a date. Our 1,000th date. Little by little, we're getting to know each other.

"Will I ever see you again?" I asked her on the front porch.

"I had fun," she said, not really answering the question.

Next week, I might ask her to dinner.

July 28, 1999

◆ ◆ ◆

It Starts With One Chore

So here we are in the frontyard, raking leaves and admiring the winter sky.

The frontyard has a total of 11 leaves. It's an L.A. yard, so we're pretty lucky to have 11 leaves. A lot of L.A. yards have far fewer leaves. Five, maybe six. But we have 11. When they all fall at once, it is something to behold.

"Look at all those leaves," the boy says, standing in the driveway, holding a rake. "Aren't they beautiful?"

They are a nice set of leaves, all right. There are a few maple, maybe a poplar or two, the rest magnolia. One leaf may actually be an old paper cup. But no one complains. When we are finished, the paper cup will give the leaf pile extra fullness.

"Maybe we can go to someone's house and take their leaves," suggests the little red-haired girl.

"Don't be greedy," I say. "Appreciate the leaves you have."

The kids are excited at the prospect of raking leaves. I have been touting the task for weeks, feeding them propaganda about how work builds character, not to mention strong, hard hands.

"Never trust a person with soft hands," I tell them.

"Why?"

"It's the sign of an idle life," I say. "Take yours, for example."

They stop to examine their hands. What they see are soft suburban hands, with little pink fingers that have never known a callus or even a blister, hands that are better suited to double-clicking a computer mouse or turning on a microwave.

In fact, until now, most of the work the kids have done has been with a computer mouse. They spend hours a day at the computer, gazing at the bouncy images the way kids used to gaze at TVs, their brains hooked on the flickering screen.

Sometimes, they even double-click in their sleep, their right hands curved as if holding a baseball. But it's a little plastic mouse they're dreaming of, not fastballs and home runs. These days, kids dream of molded plastic.

"Dad, can we start now?" the little red-haired girl asks, holding up her rake.

"Sure," I say. "But be careful. These are the only leaves we have."

As they rake, I grab a ladder and begin to take down the Christmas lights. When I get on top of the ladder, I notice that the gutters need cleaning. So I quit taking the lights down and start scooping wet leaves out of the gutter.

"What are you doing?" my lovely wife asks from the porch, staring up at the ladder.

"Cleaning the gutters."

"I thought you were taking down the Christmas lights," she says.

"That too," I say.

She stands and watches me a minute, my arms full of gutter glop.

"You sure?" she asks.

"Sure I'm sure."

She has seen this situation before, where I start some new chore before the other one is completed. Before long, there are four or five chores all going at once, all half-completed. To her, nothing is getting done. To me, everything is getting done.

"OK, whatever," she says with a sigh, disappointment sweeping across her face like an eclipse.

As she heads inside, she takes a final glance at me standing on the ladder, surrounded by gutter glop and admiring the winter sky, happy as a husband can be.

To think that it was only 15 years ago that she picked me out of a mail-order catalog, just closing her eyes and pointing at the page, which is probably as good a way as any to pick a husband.

"I'll take … that one," she said, then yelped a little when she opened her eyes to see which husband she had actually chosen.

Now, some women have been extremely lucky with mail-order husbands. But hers didn't quite live up to expectations. Like a lot of items you order by mail, her husband seemed kind of flimsy. And hard to keep clean. Worst of all, there were no refunds or exchanges.

To this day, it remains one of modern romance's great mysteries, how this terrific woman – who once had her pick of any boy in the state of Florida – wound up with a mail-order husband who finds joy in cleaning gutters and raking leaves.

"What's wrong with Mom?" the boy asks, watching her turn and go into the house.

"Buyer's remorse," I say.

"She bought a horse?" he asks, not quite hearing.

"Yeah, she bought a horse," I say, grabbing another armful of gutter glop.

Meanwhile, the little red-haired girl is finishing up the leaves. She is down to only two leaves, and she scoots them across the yard like hockey pucks, adding them to the pile one at a time, then standing back and admiring her work. Finally, she wipes her forehead and looks down at her tiny suburban hands.

"Look, Dad!" says the little red-haired girl.

"What?"

"I think I have a callus!"

"Let me see that."

I climb down the ladder and look at her hand. Sure enough, right below the second finger is a baby callus.

"Congratulations," I say. "You have your first callus."

She drops her rake and runs to show her mother.

"Hey, Mom," she yells, "I have a callus!"

As I return to the Christmas lights and the gutter glop, the boy continues to rake. Every few seconds, he stops to look at his hands. Finally, he thinks he spots something.

"Hey, Dad, I'm getting a callus too," the boy says, holding it inches from his face, studying it till his eyes cross.

"I hope it lasts forever," he says proudly.

I explain to him that sometimes the callus goes away, but the work ethic lasts. And now that he's earned his first callus, the others will come more easily.

"Thanks, Dad," he says.

January 28, 1998

◆ ◆ ◆

The Moms of Summer

THE young batter stands at the plate, squinting into the late afternoon sun, a nuclear disaster that is normally 93 million miles away but today seems to be hovering just 300 feet above the Earth, directly over right field actually, touching the trees and melting the edges of the outfield. A pitcher's sun. The orange monster.

"Tough sun," one of the mothers says.

"That might help our pitchers."

"I hope so," a mother says.

The pitchers' moms huddle tight in the bleachers. They are like those astronaut wives in "Apollo 13," thinking positive thoughts no matter what the prospects, nervously twisting their wedding bands and inhaling sharply with every windup, attempting to guide the pitch over the plate by sheer willpower.

One by one, their sons take the mound to pitch. Sometimes for three innings. Sometimes for one or two. Sometimes the boy lasts only part of an inning, giving up hit after hit before the coach walks slowly to the mound to hand the ball to a new pitcher.

"He's doing great," a woman says, trying to comfort the pitcher's mom, the mother of the moment.

"Yeah, he only gave up four runs," the pitcher's mom says grimly.

"Lucky hits," her friend says, patting her gently on the back. "All lucky hits."

Call them the Moms of Summer, the mothers whose sons go to war once or twice a week on baseball diamonds across America.

As the fathers stand stoically in the dugout, the Moms of Summer cringe with every line drive or bloop single that falls in the wrong place at the wrong time.

They sit in little clusters in the bleachers, reassuring one another and sharing things only they know. Joy. Pain. Heartbreak. Occasional contractions. Because to them, watching their sons play hardball is like the final stage of childbirth, the one they never tell you about in Lamaze class.

"Oh no, he's going to pitch," a mother says, spotting her son warming up.

"He'll do fine," another mother assures her.

"That's what you said last time," the mother says.

The mother looks at her nails, then at her son, then at her nails again.

"Don't bite your nails, Mom," her lovely and patient older daughter warns.

I know this mom pretty well. She used to work with the boy in the yard when he was younger, throwing him popups and teaching him to dive for the ball, to sail over the sprinkler heads and skid across the new sod to make great catches.

"Use two hands," she'd tell the boy. "And try not to get your clothes dirty."

And she'd throw him popups for half an hour, then half an hour more, because 30 minutes wasn't enough.

"Good catch, Mickey Mantle," she'd say, and her little boy would flip the ball back to her and trot proudly back for the next throw.

Now 12, he throws too hard for her. And the little popups she used to throw ... well, he laughs at them. Apparently he's outgrown frontyard popups.

"I want to get married on the mound," the boy told me one day recently.

"Today?" I asked.

"No, maybe in a few years," he said.

He had heard about a St. Louis pitcher who got married on the mound. So that's what he'd like to do, preferably in his uniform, preferably between games of a July doubleheader, in which he'd pitch the second game for the Dodgers – maybe striking out McGwire a couple of times – before taking off to honeymoon in Disney World.

But first he has to pitch today.

"Just throw strikes," his mother says as he takes the mound to face the other team's biggest kid.

As 12-year-olds go, the batter is a giant, broad-shouldered and tall, big as some of the dads. When he walks to the plate, steam seems to rise all around him, like it does for swamp creatures and religious resurrections.

The pitcher's mother immediately considers pulling her son out of the game and moving to North Dakota or some other cold Plains state where the baseball season lasts about five days, a place where baseball is easier on a mom.

"Just throw strikes," she calls to her son in the meantime.

The other mothers are clustered around her now, offering their support and little sips of water, hoping she'll hold up in this important game.

It is late now, about the time it was in Mudville when Casey struck out.

The Moms of Summer take note of this. At some point in their sons' baseball careers, every mother has a Casey at the plate. Or on the mound. Sooner or later in baseball, everybody fails at some key moment.

So the pitcher's mother watches through her fingers and inhales sharply with every pitch.

"Strike One!" the umpire shouts.

And for a moment, the Moms of Summer all smile.

June 24, 1998

◆ ◆ ◆

The Case of the Missing Tooth

HERE'S what happened, I'm pretty sure. I'm dreaming the sweet dream, the one with Katharine Ross at Super Bowl VII.

Midway through the second quarter, I call timeout and marry her on the spot. No tux. Just me in my Vikings uniform and her in that cotton thing she wore in "Butch Cassidy." It's a pretty common dream. Most men have it.

When suddenly, some kid awakens me from this dream and climbs into bed with us. Me and my first wife. The kid and her stupid teddy bear.

"What's wrong?"

"I lost a tooth," the little girl says, and the wife pulls back the covers.

I take the tooth, put it on the nightstand where it is safe, next to the 11 books I'm reading all at once. In minutes, I drop back to sleep, hoping to catch the third quarter and a postgame honeymoon.

No luck. The wedding is over. Katharine Ross has left me for a linebacker. The game is out of reach. The cheerleaders have stretch marks.

So I awaken to hear the dog sniffing around. He is standing on my chest and snorting around the nightstand.

He is standing with a back foot on my clavicle because it gives him better access to the baby tooth. He has a front foot on my windpipe to kill me.

Because he just ate the baby tooth. And if he doesn't kill me, he knows I'll probably kill him. Talk about your dog days. It's a dad-eat-dog world.

"Hey!" I yell too late.

So the dog swallows the baby tooth. Smiles at me. Licks his lips, like he's just been sipping Jack Daniels. Normally, he doesn't drink till later in the day.

It's the same smile Katharine Ross gave me in the dream, except the dog of course is naked. And not the least bit ashamed.

"He ate my tooth!" the little girl screams. "Mom, he ate my tooth!"

"Hey!" I yell again as the dog jumps off the bed. He was last spotted in Toledo. Headed for New York.

Actually, the little girl was pretty good about it. She cried for only two hours. I soothed her with those blueberry pancakes I make from scratch, into which her tears fell. My pancakes are largely inedible but strangely absorbent. I think it's the flour I use.

"Want some orange juice?" I ask.

"Syrup?" she says.

"I'll get the syrup," I say.

It takes me, as always, a few minutes to find the syrup in the refrigerator, even though it's generally in the same place every time, along the door with the salad dressings and the horseradish.

"There it is," I say proudly as I reach for the syrup.

"You amaze me," my wife says.

"In what sense?" I say, because I don't get that every day.

"You just amaze me," she says, shaking her head.

And I think back over the last 12 hours to figure out what I did – besides maybe finding the syrup – that was so special.

All I can remember is how in the middle of the night, the little girl lost that tooth and I put it on the nightstand. Then, first thing in the morning, the dog climbed up on my chest and ate the tooth. An hour after the crime, the wet spot on the nightstand was still wet.

"I never knew dogs ate teeth," I tell my wife.

"Only if you leave them lying around," she says.

Now, like most guys, I value emotional honestly over all else. So I say nothing. For a minute I say nothing. Sometimes silence is as honest as you can get.

"You know, if she brushed her teeth ... ," I say.

"I brush," says the little girl.

"If your teeth were cleaner, the dog wouldn't be eating them," I say.

"I brush," insists the little girl.

"You're a good brusher," I tell her.

"Thanks," she says.

She cried for only two more hours, then bounced back good as new and had some lunch, chewing on one side of her face.

Which is where we are now, at the lunch table, trying to figure out how I am amazing.

"Mom says I'm amazing," I tell the boy.

"You?"

"Yeah, me," I say.

"I think she's just joking," he says.

"But what if she's not?" I say.

"I think you need a vacation," he says.

We all need a vacation. You do. I do. Our kids do. Our dogs.

We need a vacation because our kids, softened by summer, have started behaving like the children of some third-rate monarchy. Sleepy, with a complete lack of ambition. Much like me.

We need a vacation because we just discovered that the tomato plants are sterile. Seventy-five bucks I spent to buy, plant and fertilize eight beautiful plants.

Sterile.

We need a vacation because we take the kids to see "Legally Blonde," and the ticket stub reads "Legally Blo," which somehow amuses me for days after.

"Look," I say, showing my wife the ticket stub.

" 'Legally Blo'?" she says.

"Isn't that funny?"

"No," she says.

"Oh, OK," I say.

We need a vacation because when my wife joins me in the pool, the water suddenly tastes better. Wife soup. My favorite summer dish.

We need a vacation because the dogs are eating our teeth.

"You're amazing," I tell my wife one night.

"In what sense?" she asks.

"In every sense."

"We need a vacation," she says.

August 1, 2001

◆ ◆ ◆

Mom and Dad Get Ready for Prom

IT'S 10 hours till prom, and her mother and I are discussing the prospects of attaching a LoJack sensor to our daughter's pretty prom ankle.

You know, LoJack, those anti-theft tracking devices. People put them on their BMWs. Why not on their teenage daughters? PromJack – an ankle bracelet studded with cubic zirconium.

"I could wrestle her to the ground," I tell my wife, "and you could snap the sensor to her ankle."

We end up rejecting the idea because we're not sure I could wrestle my lovely and patient older daughter to the ground. She's 17 and nimble as a race-horse.

I'd wind up chasing her around the frontyard, with her laughing and trotting at half speed while I lunged for her feet. I'd hurt myself on a sprinkler head, and the neighbors would have another story to tell. The day Prom Dad got 28 stitches in his knee.

"Maybe we'll skip the ankle bracelet," I tell my wife.

"So what'll we do?"

"Helicopter surveillance," I say.

"Good thinking."

Helicopters are easily available these days. My friend Michael says he could get us one for $575 an hour, a Bell Jet Ranger with the TV platform.

I'll hover over the hotel while the kids dine and dance, then track them when they leave.

Helicopters are so common in Los Angeles, the kids will never notice. They'll assume it's just another breaking celebrity murder and continue on with their evening.

* * *

It's six hours till prom and our lovely daughter is off to get her nails done. Just what L.A. needs – more beautiful hands and feet.

Here we are in prom season and there is an outbreak of beautiful people. First, they get their nails done. Then their hair. Then their makeup.

When my daughter speaks to me, it's almost always to ask for another check. She and her mother have worked out a plan where we pay almost all her prom expenses and our older daughter pays for almost none of them.

"That's fine with me," I say. "She can pay for college."

"Today is not the day to argue," my wife says.

"How about tomorrow then?" I ask. "Can we argue tomorrow?"

"Give her the check," her mother says.

There are times when a dad just needs to stand back and shut up. A prom is maybe one of those times. Dads become scenery at times like these. We become a birdhouse in the background.

"Thanks Daddy," my lovely and patient older daughter says, then launches into a long explanation of her next beauty procedure.

She speaks quickly, my daughter, like a Dizzy Gillespie trumpet solo, flurries of 16th notes splayed over several octaves, some of the notes garbled, others brilliant.

I don't understand such solos. Mostly, I just nod and hand over the checks.

"Nice job," my wife says as I give my daughter more money.

"Tomorrow, we talk," I say.

"Right," my wife says.

Three hours till prom and I follow my daughter to drop off her car at the expensive hotel, where they have arranged a post-prom party.

There will be a bungalow, with chips and soft drinks. Just to make sure the drinks stay soft and the prom dresses stay on, one of the mothers will be positioned in clear sight nearby.

"That's smart," I tell my wife when I hear the plan.

"I think so too," she says.

"And I can shine a spotlight," I say.

"What are you talking about?"

"From the helicopter," I say.

One hour till prom, and we're standing around with other parents in someone's nice frontyard, waiting to take pictures of the beautiful people before the limo arrives.

The moms hop here and there with cameras as the Prom Dads sort of mill around in the background, hands thrust deep in their empty pockets.

Our lovely and patient older daughter, having dressed at a friend's house, is late for pictures. I stand there like a dork, holding her corsage.

"Hey, that must be the limo," someone says.

In the street, the Queen Mary has arrived, a white 40-foot Lincoln, slurping $2-a-gallon gasoline. It would be cheaper to run the engine on champagne.

"Looks like it'd snap in half," says one of the other Prom Dads, studying the long wheelbase.

"Must have an I-beam running down the middle," I say.

Finally, our daughter arrives, dazzling as always. She was dazzling when she was born and she is dazzling now, smelling of talc and a few other things I can't really identify. Too much junk in the air. Perfume. Limo fumes. Money.

"When do I give her away?" I ask my wife.

"It's a prom, not a wedding," she tells me.

OK, now I've got that straight. Little by little, I learn about prom.

"Here, give me the camera," my wife says.

I am amazed at how beautiful these kids are. They look the way movie stars strive to look – lean as tulips, hair shimmering, skin lustrous. Frankly, they look better than movie stars.

One of the girls, a striking blond, perfect and fresh as a raindrop on a leaf, kneels down to have a picture taken with a little girl, who is dressed for the event in her Snow White costume.

It is one of those poignant, pre-prom moments. The wide-eyed 5-year-old and the wide-eyed 17-year-old. The before-and-after of a parent's life. Quick, shoot me before I melt.

"Hey, everybody in the car!" someone yells.

"OK," I say.

"Not you," my wife says.

And 18 kids climb aboard the Queen Mary. After a few moments, the limo pulls away – 18 kids buffed and polished, with everything their parents ever taught them swirling somewhere in their heads. Was it enough? Will they remember?

Probably, we'll never know.

May 16, 2001

◆ ◆ ◆

Her Great Gatsby

WE are fortunate, somehow, to live in one of those leafy Los Angeles suburbs where the burglar alarms can be mistaken for the neighing of horses, and the marriages consist almost always of strawberries and lovemaking. Or lovemaking and strawberries, depending on the couple.

Sure, there are other activities too. Laundry. Soccer. The washing of the dog, which is similar to lovemaking, what with all the kissing and ear-nibbling that goes on.

And, once in a while, there's a great party.

"So, are we having a party?" I ask, the way Gatsby used to.

"For Halloween?" my wife asks.

She and I have this arrangement, arrived at early in our marriage: I'll handle the Halloween parties. She'll handle the kids' weddings.

It's a very balanced setup. One of us winds up handling a creepy, frightening occasion where people dress up in funny clothes and misbehave. The other handles Halloween. Seems fair enough.

"I don't know about a Halloween party," my wife says. "They're a lot of work."

"Me either," says one of the kids.

"I'll take care of everything," I say.

And for a few days, I actually live up to this lie. I wash the dog. I clean the garage. I climb stepladders and hang Halloween things.

I've reached the age where if I stand on a stepladder for five minutes, the muscles in my legs begin to quiver and my potassium level drops dangerously.

Soon, the room begins to spin and I am flailing like a canary, grasping for whatever cheap crepe paper thing I just taped to the ceiling. For me, it's much like flying.

"You OK up there?" my wife asks over and over.

"I'm fine," I say.

The agreement this year is that we will have a downsized Halloween party. Not dozens of adults. Not dozens of teenagers.

Just a dozen of the little girl's friends. No stress. No mess. No police showing up on the doorstep at midnight, pleading for calm and a piece of Halloween cake.

On the menu, five large pizzas. A case of soft drinks. A few bags of chips.

"I've rented some tables," my wife says the morning of the party.

"Do we really need extra tables?"

"Where were they all going to sit?" she asks.

"Sit?" I say.

These kids won't sit. They are 9 and 10. They'll circle the house like pirates, I tell my wife. They'll chase squirrels from the trees and knock birds from the sky. They'll set fire to the furniture. It'll be fun.

"I've got this idea for a party game," I say.

"What?" the little girl asks.

"Halloween Survivor," I say. "Tribal Council, the whole deal."

"Can I be host?" the little girl asks.

"Sure," I say, "but you'll have to be funny."

"Maybe Pete should host," she says.

Which is a real kick in the chops. Pete is her friend's dad. He makes movies. He's professionally funny, in a laugh-out-loud, milk-through-your-nose sort of way. Does more dialects than the U.N.

But he's not giving the party. He's not duct-taping witches to the wall and hanging skeletons and cleaning out real spider webs from the garage to hang fake ones, $1.39 a bag.

He's not hanging orange and black streamers from the garage ceiling and accidentally stapling his thumb to the rafters. He's not missing the Nebraska-Oklahoma game, or the first three innings of the World Series, Schilling on the mound.

Pete's not doing that. In fact, on the day of the party he's taking his wife, the leggy dentist, off to Vegas for some sort of romantic, booze-filled felony that will last most of the weekend. Pete's watching football. Pete's probably having strawberries.

"Pete's booked," I tell the little girl.

"Too bad," she says.

"I could host," I tell her.

"You?" the little girl says.

Who am I, Wink Martindale? Sure, I have my limitations. But I'm completely capable of hosting a kids' party. I can entertain fifth-graders. Once, I even made my wife laugh. It was years ago, and I was probably naked at the time. But she laughed, for what seemed like hours.

"Maybe Billy Crystal's available," I tell the little girl.

"Who?" she asks.

"Or maybe I'll just host," I say.

"Whatever," she says, a ringing endorsement.

So I grab another bag of Sav-On spider webs and climb back up on the ladder. I climb back down, grab the staple gun, then climb back up. For two hours, this is pretty much how it goes.

But on the way to setting out the rental chairs, a great thing happens. I brush by my wife, who shows signs of recognition. Even interest.

"There's that Gatsby guy again," she's probably thinking.

Her hair smelled of strawberries.

October 31, 2001

◆ ◆ ◆

Hey, Softball Fans, There's a Draft in Here

THERE'S nothing like a little hot e-mail on a cold day. Something provocative. Something to get the blood racing.

Will you make the draft? Do I have to cover for you?

It's from my wife, this e-mail. A generous offer. The softball draft is in two hours, and she wants to know if I'll be home in time. If not, she'll go.

My wife has offered to go to the damp little community room and sit in a hard metal chair for two hours with a dozen other coaches to select a little-girl softball team.

I am grateful for this offer. It reveals a generous spirit and a competitive fire. No other woman has ever offered to go to a team draft for me. I remember now why I married her.

So I e-mail her back.

I may be a little late for the draft.

It's a coach's worst nightmare. Late to the team draft. Of all the things a coach can't screw up, it's the draft. The draft is where great teams are born. It can make or break your year.

How late?

Don't worry. It's really easy. An idiot could do it. But I'm tied up at work.

Who do you want me to pick?

All we really need is a shortstop, a center fielder and a couple of pitchers.

That sounds pretty easy.

We also need a left-hander at first base and a catcher who can make the throw down to second.

Draft young, mostly third-graders, and if you can't decide, then pick the kid with the parent who will be most helpful. Don't discriminate against the really attractive moms. Remember, it's not their fault.

Be sure to draft someone with a big house for the team party, preferably someone who hasn't painted the interior recently and won't mind if 12 screaming kids tear through the house like monkeys on mopeds.

See if you can get Mr. Ulf, because he tells the best jokes and his kids hit like King Kong. Mr. Rhymer would be good too because he always brings

Bazooka bubble gum.

Don't draft any whiners or anybody with the last name of Strawberry. Or a first name of Strawberry. Don't draft any Strawberrys or anybody who ever played for the Chicago Cubs.

For carpool purposes, be sure the parents all drive Suburbans or Humvees or big vegetable trucks.

I think Susan might agree to be Team Mom, so see if you can get her daughter Kaitlin in the early rounds. Don't wait on Susan. I mean Kaitlin. She could go early.

Pick mostly for athletic talent, but a good attitude is important too. If the kid has parents who appreciate a postgame margarita late on a warm spring day, that's a big plus. Maybe a priority. We didn't ask about margaritas during tryouts. My mistake. Do what you can.

Many of the girls you wouldn't recognize. They are getting really big now. Some are as tall as bar stools. They'll go in the early rounds.

But don't draft just for size. Speed is important. Aggression is important. And remember: No nose pickers.

If things go badly, see if you can work out a trade with Craig. He's an attorney and a really tough bargainer, but if you include enough players, he gets confused by all the math and you can usually sneak one or two players past him. Plus, you're pretty cute. In fact, you're really cute. You should get the best of any negotiations. Wear the blue sweater. The one you got for Christmas.

If Craig won't trade, try Dennis. He gets sleepy around 9:30. If he nods off, just reach over and grab the medical releases of any players you want. It may seem unfair. Don't worry. Coaches do this all the time.

If a trade doesn't work, collapse on the table and break into tears and complain that the other coaches are conspiring to stack their teams and playing petty political games that threaten to ruin our season and destroy our community's sports programs, which we've helped build from nothing in 20 years to where they are now, which is pretty much still nothing.

But don't tell them that. Be positive. Just cry a lot and be positive. Tell them you're from the PTA. Don't threaten them with it. Just bring it up casually. "By the way, did I mention I'm with the PTA?" Like that.

Try to get there early. If you're careful, you can sneak extra softballs out of the other teams' equipment bags and replace them with lemons and oranges from the little trees outside the front door. This will give us a psychological edge early in the season.

If someone catches you, explain that lemons and oranges are great for batting practice because no one ever has to chase them and they make really refreshing treats. Several of the newer coaches will believe you and help you fill the bags with lemons and oranges. Just smile and thank them for their help.

So, that's what we need in the draft. Do your best. Be honorable, fair and decent with the other coaches. In return, you will get nothing. That's how you'll know you're in the right place. Good luck.

I hit the send key. I wait a minute. Then another minute. I fear she's backing out. Then it arrives.

That sounds pretty easy.

It is, I write. It's not too tough.

You want me to draft a quarterback too?

I'll be right home, I say.

March 1, 2000

◆ ◆ ◆

Granite Is a Girl's Best Friend

"MOM'S making crepes," the little girl says.

"Great," I say.

"What do you like on your crepes?" she asks.

"Veal tenderloin," I say.

"OK, I'll go tell her," the little girl says, running off to place my breakfast order.

Here at our little Graceland, we love to eat. So after 20 years of marriage, some more sensational than others, I am finally giving my wife the kitchen she deserves – a place to stuff crepes and season a steak, a place to make love and school lunches.

OK, maybe not love. But every other goopy dish you crave. Here at Graceland, food is how we show affection.

"Mom's making manicotti," the little girl says.

"Yum."

"What do you want with it?" she asks.

"Milkshakes," I say.

In a week, the old kitchen will be gone. Then they'll bring in a new kitchen. It'll be like magic how quickly it all happens.

"Oh, you're renovating?" a neighbor asks after contractors deliver a gigantic dumpster.

"Yes."

"It'll be chaos," the neighbor predicts.

Thanks. But we're used to chaos. We have chaos for breakfast, along with three kinds of cereal, muffins, oatmeal, melon, fresh strawberries, Easter candy and piping-hot coffee made with this fancy new machine my wife received for Christmas.

Of course, it's not just an ordinary coffeemaker. Nothing's ordinary anymore.

"This thing takes forever to clean," I say.

"It's worth it," my wife says.

Another unsatisfying spousal reply, delivered from a foot away, by my bride of two decades – the one with the Marlo Thomas eyes. From a foot away, maybe less. In the movies, that's kissing distance.

"I don't even like coffee," I growl.

"Because you still drink Bosco," she growls back.

Ever notice the Doppler effect of marriage? The closer you get, the worse you communicate?

From a room away, we seem to get along fine. Then, as we close the distance between us, something happens to raise the tension. Train whistles blow. Bells clang. Then all marriage breaks loose.

"This coffee maker has 20 parts," I complain.

"So?"

"Where do I put this?" I say, holding up a plastic funnel.

"Don't tempt me," my wife warns.

It's a tricky project, a new kitchen. There is plumbing and electricity to deal with. Flooring. Cabinets. Lighting.

Most important, proper spacing. You don't want a kitchen so big that you're not bumping backsides. Bumping backsides is one of the little pleasures a kitchen gives. Plus it heightens the illusion of togetherness that is so important in a modern relationship.

"Hey, quit bumping me," I tell her.

"You're bumping me," my bride says.

"If you insist," I say.

Along the counter, like squares of toast, my wife has placed several little pieces of granite. They're samples for the new granite countertops we're considering, more stuff we can't afford.

To this day, I'm not sure how we managed to afford this tiny house in the leafy suburb, let alone this renovation. We're probably paying in manicotti. With side orders of crepes.

"I think I like the dark gray," my wife says, tilting her head as she studies the granite samples. "You?"

"Yellow Formica," I say.

To me, there's nothing really wrong with the current kitchen. Built in 1443, it has a scruffy charm. Pirates once owned it. For a while, it housed sheep. Then a couple who subscribed to Car & Driver magazine.

After 500 years, the kitchen now smells of scrambled eggs even when we're not having scrambled eggs. It takes centuries of bad breakfasts to acquire a smell like that. The patina on our Acropolis.

"Maybe I like this one," my wife says, studying a second granite sample.

"Perfect," I say. "We'll look like the Luxor."

"This is serious," she says rather seriously.

19

Yes, this is serious. It's serious because our friends Hank and Martha have granite countertops. Don and Kate, too. Everyone seems to have granite countertops, and if we don't get some soon, some other new surface might come along and we'd miss out on this unnecessary but expensive trend. Granite, the stuff of kitchen counters and tombstones.

"I love Bill and Nancy's counters," says my wife.

"Bill's a Republican," I say, explaining the various caste systems involved.

"And Nancy doesn't work," she reminds me.

Yes, but my wife does. So I guess she's going to get her granite countertops. Hank and Martha. Bill and Nancy. Don and Kate. The whole world's gone granite. Why not us?

Because here at Graceland, granite is how we show affection.

April 10, 2002

◆ ◆ ◆

Dates on Tape

SO imagine you're on a first date, and it's going really well, and you're able to stop the date – just call "date timeout" – and project you and your companion 10 years into the future.

"What's 'date timeout'?" my wife asks.

"That's when you stop the date, right in the middle, and you call timeout," I explain.

"How many timeouts would you get?" she asks.

"Two," I say.

And I explain how during the timeout, a video crew would roll a big TV into the restaurant and play a tape of the two of you 10 years in the future.

In this preview of your life, you'd just be doing normal things, like helping with homework or cleaning up after the dog or putting eardrops in the baby's ear, while the baby wails and the dog gets sick again and the phone rings and a nurse you've never met chirps, "Congratulations, you're going to have another baby." Just normal everyday stuff like that. Nothing major.

"And you'd get to see how the other person handles it?" my wife asks.

"Exactly," I say.

I say "exactly" because that's what everybody says these days. You can't go through a conversation without one of the participants answering a statement with "exactly." Know what I'm saying? Exactly.

And I tell my wife that if you liked what you saw in this date timeout, liked the video pre-play of your life together, that you could then go on a second date. On the second date, if things were going well, you could call another "date timeout," then project the two of you 20 years in the future.

"Twenty years?" she asks.

"Exactly," I say.

"Yikes," she says.

I don't know what she means by "yikes." We're almost 20 years into our marriage and having dinner in a nice Pasadena restaurant. There are no yikes about it. It is all too nice.

Of course, we can't usually afford the nice Pasadena restaurants. But this one comes courtesy of a gift certificate from the softball team. There is wine. On our plates, $6 salads.

"Great salad," I say.

"Mine too."

A guy comes by with the pepper grinder. My date declines, but I ask for extra. For 18 years, our dinner dates have been just like this. Pepper never touches her salad plate but falls in giant heaps on mine – almost in dunes – till people three tables away begin to sneeze in their soup.

"You eat too much pepper," she always says.

"I'm trying to cut back," I always respond.

For the main course, scallops.

"Great scallops," I say.

"Mine too," my date says.

They do great things with scallops at this restaurant. They spread six or seven of them around the huge plate. Like a spa, this plate – a hot spa of butter, garlic and scallops.

But that's not all. In the middle of the plate is a mound of mashed potatoes with a large architectural device, possibly a giant piece of cereal, maybe Wheat Chex, resting right in the potatoes.

I stare at the Wheat Chex. It looks like a spinnaker there in the potatoes, ready to catch a gust of wind and return these scallops to the ocean where they belong.

"What's this?" I ask my wife, nodding at the Wheat Chex.

"It's lovely," she says.

"Can I eat it?"

"You ate your parsley, didn't you?" she says.

As our dinner progresses, I try to talk her into pretending this is our first date.

She thinks this is a particularly dopey suggestion. If this were the 1950s, she'd blow a cloud of cigarette smoke in my face and check her watch. Pull lint from her sleeve. Make eye contact with the bartender. Like many men, I would find this appealing.

"OK, go ahead," she finally says, daring me to be date-like.

"So tell me about yourself," I say.

"Me, there's not much to tell," she says.

"Try me," I say.

"Well, I've got three kids, a dog, a cat and an orange-bellied frog," she says.

"Money's tight?" I say.

"Exactly," she says. "I spend my weekends at soccer fields, my nights helping with homework and my free time scrubbing vomit stains off the carpet."

"So life is good?" I say.

"Can't complain," she says. "So tell me about you."

I tell her how I once invented the street curb and some years later, the harvest moon. Just thought of it all at once, as a way to improve autumn evenings.

"That's very interesting," she lies and checks her watch.

"I'm also a very wealthy man," I say.

"Street curbs?" she asks, pulling lint from her sleeve.

"No, baseballs," I say. "I'm rich with baseballs. I keep them in buckets in the garage."

"So life is good?" she says.

"Can't complain," I say.

While we're eating, she gives me one of her scallops. I take this as a good sign. Under the table, I gently bump her knee. Knee contact, an indicator of good things to come.

"Can I see you again?" I ask.

"Not in a million years," she says.

"How's tomorrow?" I ask.

"I think I'm free," she says.

Finally, dessert arrives. Like always, we share a spoon.

August 30, 2000

♦ ♦ ♦

That's the Way the Wedding Ring Bounces

WHEN we were kids, we used to drill the insides out of nickels, then pound the edges flat to make rings that quickly turned our fingers green, usually overnight.

"Wanna wear my ring'?" we'd ask skinny neighbor girls who'd watched us murder the nickels through the basement window.

"Will it turn my finger green?" the girls would ask.

"Only if you sweat," we'd say, and they'd wear the ring for a week or less, until they got a better offer from a better guy. Like an ID bracelet or a stick of gum. But as rings went, it was a good investment. In time, the green went away.

The next time I put on a ring was in a little Lutheran church in South Florida, on a steamy day in May, with 100 people in attendance, some of whom

I actually knew.

"Wanna wear my ring?" I asked the skinny girl who was by my side that day.

"Sure," she said.

She slipped the ring on her finger and handed me one too.

"Wanna wear my ring?" the skinny girl asked.

"Sure," I said.

It was a nice ring, flat and functional, a simple gold band not much fancier than the nickel rings we used to pound out in our fathers' workshops. But it felt strange, this ring. Like a blister or a fresh scar. Something funny to the touch.

"Where's your ring?" my wife would often ask through our first years of marriage.

Back then, I'd take the ring off, then forget to put it back on. It would get lost amid the spare change on the dresser. Or fall into some drawer, where it would pop up later.

"Hey, my ring," I'd say excitedly when it would turn up in the bottom of a sock. And my wife would shake her head and ask me why I didn't wear the ring more often.

"I'll get used to it," I'd promise.

For years, I tried to get used to the ring. When I'd sit idly, I would twist the ring on my finger. Sometimes, I'd slip it off and flip it in the air like a coin, trying to make the ring fun, trying to make a game of it.

Once, while heading down an escalator, I flipped the ring in the air, then took my eye off of it at the last second. It was a play I'd made a million times before. This time, the ring got away from me.

The ring pinged down the escalator – six, eight, a dozen times – singing high and clear each time it hit one of the metal steps. Ping. Ping. Ping.

For miles, you could hear it singing down the escalator. After a while, the singing stopped.

"Uh-oh," I said, or some equivalent – whatever a husband says when he sees his whole wife flash before his very eyes.

"What's wrong?" someone asked.

"Nothing," I said. "I just died, that's all."

I went to the bottom of the escalator, hoping for a miracle. Most marriages have at least one or two miracles embedded in them, waiting for the right moment. This was my moment. The wedding band was lying just past the bottom of the escalator, 40 feet from where it first fell.

"Whew, that was close," I said, before flipping the ring in the air and slipping it back on my finger.

Then came the span of four or five years when I hardly wore the ring at all. I was working long hours renovating our first house, slinging circular saws and pipe wrenches.

"Where's your ring?" my wife would ask.

And I'd tell her how guys don't like to wear rings around power tools, because the ring can snag a board or the tool itself, causing serious injury. Not only could I lose the ring but the finger too. And then how would I ever count to 10?

Besides, at any given moment, most men are married to more than one thing. They're married to their wives. They're married to their jobs. They're married to their golf games. For five years, I was married to this house, a giant Victorian that had withstood hurricanes and termites and years of neglect. And now me, trying to make it well again.

"Where's your ring?" my wife would ask.

Eventually, we moved on, leaving behind the old house and the power tools.

I started wearing the ring again. I twisted it and flipped it in the air and caught it every time, even on escalators. In time, it felt more comfortable. Sort of like a marriage. In time, I was wearing it every day, slipping it off only at night.

It's a little snug now, this ring. So far, it has not turned my finger green. So far, it has been a good investment.

One day, I suspect, I will slip it on and not be able to get it off, having finally grown into this ring I've had for 16 years.

Someday, the grandchildren will climb on my lap, then twist the ring and try to pry if off my fat finger. Only it won't come off. It'll finally be part of my hand.

"Give me your ring," they'll say as we roughhouse on the couch.

"Can't," I'll say. "It's on there for good."

February 3, 1999

CHAPTER TWO

THE OLDER DAUGHTER

♦ ♦ ♦

Welcome to Dad's School of Driving

SHE spins around the Rose Bowl parking lot in her mother's white minivan, a car with the handling and sex appeal of a giant Tupperware container. Safe. Solid. Easy to wash. Tupperware.

"I like this car," my lovely and patient older daughter says.

"Me, too," I say.

Just turned 16, my daughter hears the call of the concrete, the whistle of the automobile ads. Not once has she spotted a vehicle she wouldn't love to marry. To her, there are no ugly cars.

"Look at that nice Ford Escort," she says, as we circle the Rose Bowl parking lot.

"Very nice," I say.

We have been coming to the Rose Bowl like this for months now, spending warm summer evenings practicing her turns and stops in the giant parking lot, which leaves plenty of margin for error.

"Two hands on the wheel," I tell her.

"OK, Dad," she says.

Mostly, she's got this two-hands thing down now. When she first got her permit, she'd occasionally dangle her left arm out the window, as if holding a beer or a cigarette, which is a fine way to drive if you happen to live in Alabama and have tattoos of naked women up and down your arm. But not for her. For her, it's two hands on the wheel.

"You never know when a tire's going to blow out," I tell her.

"You don't?" she asks.

"No, you don't," I say.

Round and round the Rose Bowl lot we go, which is empty except for all the other new drivers and their dads using the parking lot for practice. Five, six, eight of them, all stopping and starting, stopping and starting.

"Look, there's Marie!" my daughter yells, then screams and waves out the window to her friend Marie, who screams and waves back.

"Two hands," I say.

"I can't believe I saw Marie," she tells me.

The student drivers and their dads prowl the giant parking lot like U-boats, wary of the other student drivers, pulling up along the curbs, then pulling out again, always with the turn signal.

At some point, all the U-boats end up in one corner of the giant parking lot, a fleet of U-boats, gridlocked in the corner.

"Don't panic," I say.

"Should I back up?" my daughter asks anxiously.

"Let's see what the others do," I say.

Apparently, the other fathers are waiting too, because for a minute, we all sit there, expecting the other U-boats to make the first move. Finally, we all decide to back up at the same time.

"That was fun," my daughter says, when we're free of the others.

"I'll never forget it," I tell her.

Used to be, driving was taught in high schools, by football coaches who could barely fit into the mid-size sedans – big men, 6 feet tall by 6 feet wide, without an ounce of fat on them.

"Both hands," they'd tell the driver, then look down to study some off-tackle slant in the playbook on their lap.

Now it's moms and dads who do the dirty work – big men and women without an ounce of fat on them – trying to sit calmly in the passenger seat while their children try to remember which pedal is the brake.

"OK, now put your foot over the brake," my wife says as they head toward a stop sign.

"Which one's the brake?" our daughter asks.

"Don't joke," her mother says sternly.

Like a lot of parents, her mother is a calm driving instructor, maintaining her composure no matter what.

"Slow down," she says as our daughter approaches a busy intersection. "Slow down. . . . Slow Down! . . . SLOW DOWN!!!"

"Chill, Mom," our daughter says when she finally slows down.

"Hey, look, there's Brittany!" she yells, waving out the window.

So when our older daughter has a choice, she prefers that her dad teach her to drive. Dads generally have a different approach to driver's ed. Dads just scream internally.

Last month, as my daughter approached her first freeway onramp, I developed a severe facial tic that eventually spread to my chest and abdomen.

And in the night, I wake up kicking at the bed sheets, looking for a brake pedal as we go speeding through an intersection in a giant white Tupperware container.

"Slow down. Slow Down! SLOW DOWN!!!" I scream in my dreams.

"It's OK," my wife says when she wakes me.

"That was close," I say.

"You can let go of my hair now," she says.

"Thanks," I say. "I think your hair saved my life."

"Then let go of it," she says.

"OK," I say.

July 14, 1999

◆ ◆ ◆

What It's Really Like at Our House

So I say to my dad, "Hey, Dad, how about I write your column this week?" and he says, "Sure, I could use a little rest," then rolls over and goes back to sleep.

He seems pretty busy, my Dad, but he's not. Mostly, he spends time explaining things to my mom, like why he keeps leaving sunflower seeds in his pockets that end up in the washing machine. Each baseball season, they have this argument.

"Why are there sunflower seeds in the washing machine?" Mom asks.

"Maybe they were dirty," my dad says.

"No more seeds!" my mom says, sounding like a policeman. And Dad takes the seeds she washed and puts them back in his pocket.

Things get pretty weird around here sometimes. Mom's, like, this really busy person. My lovely and patient older dad isn't. So there's, like, this conflict all the time over who needs to do certain stuff.

"Sure, I could install the ice maker," he says, "but who's going to watch the Dodger game?"

Which doesn't make her laugh like he thinks it will.

"I guess I'm installing an ice maker," he mumbles, then turns off the TV and goes to the garage.

This is how he does stuff. First he goes to the garage. Then he goes to the hardware store. Then he goes back into the garage. Then he goes to the bathroom for, like, an hour. Then he goes back to the hardware store. That's my dad. Always on the move.

"Be back in a minute," he says, then runs out and buys lumber or propane.

It's pretty clear he's just stalling when he runs around like this. Mom calls it his "prevent defense." I call it stalling.

"Gotta get some more anchor bolts," he says, then disappears. For 10 years, he's been buying anchor bolts.

My little sister, she's not much better. She thinks Dad is so cool. She and the dog follow him around and watch him do stuff, and sometimes they go to the hardware store with him, all three of them, to buy drill bits or grass seed or whatever.

31

"Mom, gotta get some anchor bolts!" my sister yells, and off they go.

Mom says he's turning my younger sister into a little wise guy, her hanging around him so much. Mom says he's not a very good influence on her, which is probably pretty true.

"She's turning into such a wise guy," my mom keeps saying.

"Yeah, isn't it great?" says my dad, all proud and stuff.

"We don't need more wise guys," she says.

My little sister isn't the only one. My brother, he's a wise guy, too. He constantly drives me crazy, especially when I have friends over, so sometimes we tie him up and stuff him in the couch, which makes Mom sort of mad.

"Don't stuff your brother in the couch!" she yells. "And untie him too."

It's pretty funny if you ever saw it.

I don't know if you know this, but Dad says the reason we moved to California was so my mom could be a big star, "like Greta Garbo or Goldie Hawn," whoever they are.

He says the plan was for Mom to have her own TV show so he could be a trophy husband and never have to work again, just manage her career and get first-class dental care, which is what the husbands of movie stars mostly do, he says.

What happened, I guess, is that by the time they got to California, they already had two kids, me and my brother, and one more on the way. So it was hard for her to go out on auditions, all pregnant and waddling like a duck and stuff.

"CBS was interested for a while," my dad says. "Then her water broke."

I think he's kidding, but you can never tell with him. He's always making jokes.

"It's too bad because she's pretty talented," he always says, then pinches my mom on the backside, and she jumps and they horse around in the kitchen like they're young again, grabbing each other's wrists. It's so gross. Believe me, it's even more sickening when you see it. Yuck. I guess when you're married, you get pretty desperate.

Parents today can be so strange. I swear they are the dullest people I ever met and they just happen to be my family. How unlucky is that? I mean, I love them and everything, except they drive me crazy.

Sometimes, I talk about how in two more years I'll be going away to college and that I need to start visiting some places, which makes Dad kind of grumpy and he grinds his teeth and doesn't want to talk about it.

My friends say their dads grind their teeth too. Mom says that's what men do instead of talking. Grind their teeth.

"She's 16," my mom reminds him.

"Who's 16?" he says.

"Your first daughter," she explains, meaning me.

"No way," he says, and he gets this faraway look in his eyes like he's watching a baseball game on TV, or searching the horizon for ships.

"Sixteen?" he mumbles.

He looks like a puppy when he gets like this, kind of old, but like a puppy, if you know what I mean. An old puppy.

Mom calls it his "Walter Matthau look," whoever that is, some old movie star or maybe he was president, I forget.

They talk in code sometimes, my parents. Whenever they whisper, I can tell when something really good happened, like some uncle got arrested or somebody had a baby who wasn't legally supposed to. I know that stuff happens. Even in our family.

Which is why we really moved to California, I think.

Other than that, things are pretty dull around here. I hope this wasn't too boring. Who knows, in the future, I might have an ice maker to tell you about. Just don't hold your breath.

April 19, 2000

◆ ◆ ◆

The Night Before Christmas

THE little boy is standing over my bed like a drunk at a buffet table, tired and teetering, ready to fall face first at any moment.

"Dad?"

His voice is way up high in his throat, even higher than usual. Apparently he just had a nightmare.

"Go back to bed," I say.

"But, Dad . . . "

I know I shouldn't do it. Because if you let a kid in bed with you for one night, you've got him there all year. But it's cold. And it's Christmastime, the season for taking in stragglers.

"Thanks, Dad."

He settles in next to me, all elbows and knees, which jab at me like broom handles.

"You OK?" I ask.

"Yeah."

I go back to where I was when he arrived, in that place in my head that worries about money. It's almost Christmas, too late to worry about money. But I worry anyway.

Just as I'm about to fall asleep, I hear it again.

"Dad?"

This voice doesn't belong to the boy. It's much lower.

"Dad?" his little sister says again.

"What's the story, morning glory?" I ask.

"I can't sleep."

Five minutes later, the older sister arrives. And suddenly, at 1:15 in the morning, I'm sleeping with the enemy.

"Not a peep," I warn them. "Not a peep or it's back to your rooms. All three of you."

"Peep," my son says.

"You, out!" I say.

"Sorry, sorry, sorry," he says.

They are wedged between my wife and me, with their arms to their sides, staring at the ceiling and breathing through their mouths.

In December, all kids breathe through their mouths. That's because in December, all kids have colds. Christmas colds. In fact, the president just declared December "Mucus Appreciation Month."

So as my three mouth-breathers drift off to sleep, I go back to that place in my head that worries about money. There is still no money there, but I go back anyway.

Then it happens.

"What's that?" the youngest one asks.

"What?" I say.

"I heard something," she says.

There's that pause you get whenever a bunch of people stop to listen for something. As usual, no one hears a thing.

"Go to sleep," her brother grumbles.

"Dad, I really heard something," the 5-year-old insists. "It sounded like . . . like Santa."

"What?"

"I think he's checking on us," she says, breathless with excitement.

"To see if we're naughty or nice?" her older sister gently teases.

"Yup," the 5-year-old says.

Her 10-year-old brother reacts with a scoffing noise in the back of his throat that sounds roughly like someone gagging on a piece of roast beef. This gagging sound has more meaning than an actual word because if conveys pure skepticism like no word can.

"I heard it too," I say.

"See," the 5-year-old says.

"Dad?" the 13-year-old says.

"Yes, honey?"

"Grow up."

I grew up a long time ago, but I haven't quite given up on Santa. That's because my 5-year-old hasn't quite given up on Santa.

Some in the family consider the two of us extremists. Others just think we're dopes. The truth is probably somewhere in the middle.

"Dad, tell me again," says the 10-year-old. "How does Santa visit a billion homes in one night?"

"Yeah, Dad," says the 13-year-old. "And how does he get past all those home security systems?"

Tough crowd. In the old days, I could read them "The Night Before Christmas" and that was all they needed to know. Then a couple of years later, I reluctantly reported that "Yes, Virginia, there is a Santa Claus."

"Santa exists as surely as hope and reason and MTV," I told them, improvising just a little.

But pure faith isn't enough anymore. The older ones insist on facts. And for some reason, they believe they have me trapped in a lie.

"Ever heard of Einstein?" I ask.

"Yes."

"Ever heard of the theory of relativity?" I ask.

"No."

"Then lie back and let me tell you about Santa Claus."

With this, the 13-year-old attempts to bolt. But she is trapped under the covers. Too bad. My leg is right in the way.

"Dad!"

"So according to Einstein, here's how Santa does it," I begin, reciting an explanation I found in a newspaper article last year.

"According to the theory of relativity, under the right conditions, time can dilate and space contract."

"Huh?" says the 10-year-old.

"Let me out!" cries the 13-year-old.

"On December 24," I continue, "Einstein's theory of relativity is fulfilled at the North Pole, the center of the Earth's rotation and the point of convergence of its electromagnetic field.

"When this happens, a rip develops in the fabric of time, allowing Santa to slip through. Until he comes back through the rip, time stands still. This allows him as much time as he needs to deliver packages around the world."

I pause a moment to let this last part sink in.

"Any questions?"

There's complete silence. I'm beginning to think I've won them over. Or at least confused them, which of course is the essence of persuasion.

"Dad, they're asleep," says the 13-year-old.

We lie there a little longer, me and the teenager. It seems like yesterday when she herself was 5 years old. Back then, she believed everything her father said.

Now, nearly in high school, she has become the village skeptic. But that's

OK. I love skeptics. I just wish they wouldn't grow up so fast.

"Dad," she says, breaking the silence.

"What, honey?"

"I heard something," she says.

"What?"

"It sounded like . . . like . . . "

"Go ahead, say it."

"It sounded like Santa."

I hit her with a pillow. She hits me back.

"Thanks, honey."

" 'Night, Dad."

December 24, 1996

◆ ◆ ◆

Here's My Beef

WHEN we last saw my dad, he was heading off to Porterville with his friend Irv to buy steaks, like some sort of red meat solstice.

"If it moos, cook it," that's my dad's motto.

Dad says summer's coming and he needs to stock up on T-bones and all this other weird steak stuff for the grill. Porterhouse. Ground beef. Chuck.

"Hey, Dad, who's Chuck?" I ask him.

"Don't be a wise guy," he says.

"Dad, I'm a girl."

"Don't be a wise-guy girl," he says, then turns the column over to me, the patient older daughter, as he heads off to this butcher shop.

"Hey, Mom, at least he's not shooting anything," I tell my mom.

"Not that we know about," my mom says.

You should've heard them talking. First, Mom says, "Why are you going all the way to Porterville?" And Dad says, "Do we really need a new septic tank?" And Mom says, "Soccer sign-ups are Thursday." And Dad says, "SOCCER SIGN-UPS!" like that, because soccer season just ended and already he's writing checks.

"I'm hemorrhaging money," he says.

"Oh, by the way, my car needs new tires," Mom says.

"Somebody help me!" he yells.

"Why, Daddy?" my little sister asks.

"Because I'm hemorrhaging money!" he says.

"Oh," says my little sister, and everybody goes back to what they were doing before.

As you know, there's not much yelling allowed in the suburbs. Usually what happens is people just internalize their frustrations, then seethe awhile, then go on with their yardwork or drive around in their SUVs until everything's normal again. I swear, I am so looking forward to college.

Sometimes Dad will just be sitting there watching "The Three Stooges" on TV and going, "Curly Howard was a genius. A real genius," and Mom will be standing there, watching him watch "The Three Stooges."

"Come watch awhile," he'll say, and Mom will go over and sit next to him.

"I think," my dad will say, "that watching 'The Three Stooges' makes you a better parent."

"Why's that?" my brother asks.

"We have three kids," Dad says. "You do the math."

"Oh, my God!" I scream.

And my dad and brother start going "n'yuck, n'yuck, n'yuck," like that, and making Stooges sounds.

And my Mom will say, "Is this all you're going to do today – lie here on the couch?"

Which is when Dad explains to her that he's at that age where he can't think unless he's lying down.

"Einstein was that way," he says. "Especially on weekends."

"He was?" my little sister asks.

"You bet," my dad says.

"Hey, Einstein, want a sandwich?" my mom says. "Sure," says my dad, as if he'd ever turn down a sandwich.

Isn't that romantic? I love when Mom calls him Einstein.

Last weekend they argued for 30 minutes about gas prices. I swear, gas prices. And my cell phone bill. After that, they spent an hour discussing which kind of lettuce to have with dinner. Iceberg or romaine? Iceberg or romaine? Like that.

My dad says he's like the Billy Crystal of our particular suburb and my mom's his Meg Ryan, and one day they are destined to meet and fall in love all over again, soon as he quits hemorrhaging money. Soon as he gets back from Porterville.

"Why Porterville?" is what you're probably asking. I don't really know. I guess his friend Irv knows a great butcher shop up there or something.

Plus, Dad says sometimes guys just need to go off somewhere by themselves for a while, which, he says, is what led to the entire Apollo space program, not to mention Lewis and Clark and a bunch of other dead guys.

"Without wanderlust, there would be no America," he says. "There would be no Super Bowl."

Dad says if guys didn't need to get away for a while, we'd all still be living in Europe and no one would have satellite TV or democracy or Lee Marvin movies or all the things that make life worthwhile.

"Without wanderlust, there would be nothing new," he says.

So off he goes to Porterville, humming the theme from "MASH," which is the other thing he watches besides the Stooges. Mom says "MASH" used to be a big hit, like a million years ago when dad was young.

"Hey, Dad, what are you getting in Porterville?" my little sister asks.

"For you, a nice porterhouse," my dad says. "Big as a hubcap."

"Really?" my sister says, all excited and stuff.

"Maybe a mastodon steak," he says.

"Big as a hubcap?" she asks.

"Bigger," he says.

Oh, my God. Now you see what my life is like?

I don't know exactly where Porterville is, but it must be pretty far from L.A. on account of the way Dad got the car all ready and checked the oil.

When Mom asked him where it was, he says Porterville is about a million oil rigs east of Bakersfield.

"Then you take a right," he says, whatever that means. That's the way he talks around Irv. Guy talk and lots of jokes nobody gets.

And that's when we last saw my dad, heading off in the minivan, off to discover America and buy steaks, which leaves me writing his stupid column for him.

When he gets back, he says he'll grill up some steaks and make these humongous baked potatoes for everybody.

"Big as footballs," he says when he describes the potatoes.

"Bigger," says Irv.

"Bigger than footballs," my dad says.

Then he and Irv will probably sit down on the couch and watch "The Three Stooges."

I keep telling Mom that I'm pretty sure I'm never getting married. But she says I should try it eventually. By then, maybe men will be different.

"You can't judge all men by your father," she says.

"You're sure?" I say.

"Some are worse," she says.

Oh, my God.

May 2, 2001

◆ ◆ ◆

Dreams and Mirages in the Desert

Go east, young man. Forget all that Manifest Destiny stuff you heard in high school. Forget Horace Greeley. Go east. The west is full up. Go east before it's too late.

"Where we going, Dad?"

"East," I say as I ease our proud, white minivan onto Interstate 10.

Sinatra knew it. So did Cary Grant. Like us, they went west, then found it a little congested and decided to head east again. They wound up in Palm Springs, where we are today for lunch. You could die here at this crosswalk before the light turns.

"Where we going now?" someone asks.

"Across the street for lunch," I say.

"Whoa," the little girl says, like she never crossed the street before.

We are on the road again, like Steinbeck and Kuralt and every long-distance trucker you ever saw, on the road to places far off and glittery in the night, Palm Springs being our first stop.

It's nice here in the desert. Friendly. Slightly slower. Should you hesitate when the light turns green, as tourists often do, the locals don't honk at you instantly. They wait, then pass out leaning against the horn. Personally, I prefer it this way.

"I've never been to Palm Springs," the boy says.

"Me neither," I say.

For lunch, we stop at a little sidewalk cafe, where they serve a nice chicken Caesar and the sort of sandwiches that don't get all over your face and hands, the way a good sandwich should. Here, they serve neat sandwiches that taste a little too much like cardboard.

"How's your sandwich?" someone asks.

"Terrific," I say.

"Don't you love the bread?" my wife asks.

"Sure."

There is lots to do here in Palm Springs. As we eat, my lovely and patient older daughter quizzes us with Trivial Pursuit cards, left on every table in the restaurant.

"What's an integrated circuit mainly made of?" she asks.

"Silicon."

"What name has been used by the most popes?" she asks.

"Ringo?" I say.

"John," she says with a laugh. "You were close, Dad."

We are headed east to look at colleges for her, so she has a right to be giddy and full of life. First of all, she's full of life. Second, she's looking at colleges. Only picking out a prospective spouse or a new boat could be more exciting.

"What's the name of the tall cap worn by bishops?" she asks from the next Trivial Pursuit card.

"A fez?"

"A miter," she says.

She has outgrown us, my older daughter. Hard to figure, because, like most families, we are constantly changing – evolving, becoming more complex and interesting.

Still, my 17-year-old finds us too predictable. Too stodgy. Our hearts beat too slowly for her. Our clothes are too old.

When we walk after lunch, my lovely and patient older daughter prefers to stroll 10 paces in front. Which makes it hard for me to hold her hand.

"Why does she walk way up there?" I ask my wife.

"I don't know," she says. "Maybe she's trying to ditch us."

Who would ditch us? Me, with my floppy Pete Maravich socks and Docker shorts. Her brother, who can lick ice cream off the tip of his nose and often does. Her little sister, singing too loudly as we walk. Who would want to leave such a family?

"She's so beautiful," I say to my wife as we walk along the Palm Springs sidewalk.

"Who?" my wife asks, lost in a real estate brochure.

"Never mind," I say.

We are so smitten with Palm Springs, we consider looking for a home here. My wife thumbs through the local real estate brochure, "Distinctive Homes of the Desert," which is just the kind of home we always look for. Distinctive.

There are three homes that appeal to us right from the start. The first one belonged to Elvis Presley. It has four bedrooms and seven baths.

"This beautiful home was one of only two homes owned by Elvis at the time of his death," the brochure brags.

The second home that catches our eye belonged to Cary Grant, a cozy 6,000-square-foot place that, the brochure says, "is a replica of a 19th century Spanish Andalusian farm house."

"One can imagine former owner Cary Grant enjoying the peaceful grounds with his third wife, Betsy Drake," the brochure claims.

The third estate is the "Frank Sinatra Compound."

"That's the one for us," I tell my wife.

"But you haven't even seen it," she says.

Turns out, I was right. Barbecue pit. Pool. Spa. Tennis court. Basketball court. Two-hole golf course. On a two-hole course, I might finally break 80.

"What are they asking?"

"It's offered at $2.3 million," she says.

"So they might take less," I say.

My wife suggests we buy the Frank Sinatra Compound and turn it into a bed-and-breakfast honoring the great singer's life.

I'd dress like Peter Lawford. She could be Mia Farrow. We'd offer special Rat Pack weekends.

There'd be an Ocean's Eleven lounge. An Ava Gardner suite. Happy hour would begin about noon. On Saturday nights, big dance bands would play in the

Tommy Dorsey Room.

"You could be Joey Bishop," I tell the boy.

"I want to be Joey Bishop," the little girl says.

"No, you're Sammy," I say.

"I am?" she says.

"You're definitely Sammy," I say with a wink.

"Oh, my God," sighs my lovely and patient older daughter from 10 paces in front.

It tells you something about our life together that this bed-and-breakfast idea isn't even the silliest thing my wife and I have ever dreamed up.

"You think it's zoned for it?" I ask.

"Zoning is for poor people," she says.

"It is?"

"Sure," she says.

We walk silently for a while, thinking about this Sinatra thing. Crazy as it sounds, we could probably do it. Except for one little detail.

"I just remembered," I say.

"What?"

"We're poor people," I say.

"Oh, that's right," she says.

On the way out of Palm Springs, I turn the wrong way on a one-way street, which puts me in prime position to be yelled at by a local on a bicycle.

"Hey, that's one-way!" the old woman on the bicycle screams. "That street's one-way!"

So I curse softly and turn the car around. East I go. The direction of our dreams.

February 28, 2001

◆ ◆ ◆

College Search 101

SO here we are touring our first college campus, a dusty little place that's home to 40,000 students in the warm bosom of the Arizona desert. During the day, there are Harry Chapin songs on the radio. At night, a distant train whistle. Not a bad place to send someone you love.

"Arizona State is a dry campus," our tour guide announces, stunning everyone in our little tour group, most notably the kids who are planning to go here. "There is no liquor allowed in the dorms."

That is not the only stunning thing our tour guide tells us. She gives us impressive stats about National Merit scholars. SAT scores. Grade point averages.

By the middle of the tour, I am fairly convinced that Arizona State is now a member of the Ivy League.

That would mean ASU is the first Ivy to be located in the middle of a desert, which seems strange to me, since most Ivy League schools tend to be clustered on the East Coast.

"Over there, that's the engineering building," our student tour guide says proudly.

We wander through the large but comfortable campus. Off to the left, there is a giant hall designed by Frank Lloyd Wright. In the middle of the campus, an impressive student center. Everywhere you look, lots and lots of bikes.

"This," our tour guide says, "is the Hugh Downs School of Human Communications."

For a moment, I think she is kidding.

"This is where I'm going," my older daughter whispers.

"It is?"

"Yes," she says. "It's very good."

With a name like that, it ought to be. Friendly and apple-cheeked, Hugh Downs has been on TV more often than Bugs Bunny. If anybody knows about human communication, it's Hugh Downs.

"This is where I go," our well-spoken tour guide says.

"That seals it for me," I tell my daughter.

To me, a college campus is almost indescribably special, special in the way that ballparks and mountain streams are special.

There is hope here. Idealism. Clear-eyed optimism about the future. If you're not careful, you could gag on it.

"Do you like it, Daddy?" my older daughter asks when our tour of ASU is over.

"It's terrific," I say.

"He doesn't like it," she tells her mother.

"Your dad just wants you to keep your options open," her mother explains.

"I do?"

"Yes," my wife says. "You do."

Things have changed on college campuses since you and I went. For one, there is electricity now. For another, college has become slightly more expensive.

I flinch like Rodney Dangerfield every time the subject of money comes up. Fees. Room and board. Books. Expenses.

The very idea of out-of-state tuition gives me back spasms. My head jerks to the left. My head jerks to the right. By the time we get to the cost of student housing, I look like a guy being attacked by crows.

"You OK, Dad?" someone asks.

"Fine," I say, my arms flailing at imaginary bankers.

In the afternoon, we take a break and watch the ASU women's tennis team take on Harvard, one of its bigger Ivy League rivals.

It's sunny, about 70. The air, perfect. Fifty or 60 fans have shown up for the match.

"Go, Devils!" the Sun Devil fans warble.

"Go, De-villlllllls!" Like that, they say it, with the accent on the second syllable and rising like a piccolo.

It's pretty clear from the start that the Harvard women are going to have a long afternoon here in Tempe – not so much because of their more skillful opponents but because of this incessant "Go, Devils" cheer they hear over and over again.

"Go, De-villlllllls!"

The ASU players are tanned and seemingly more fit, with hair spun of copper and gold. You're right, I would never describe male athletes this way. Because their hair would never be spun quite like this.

The Harvard women tend to be thicker and sturdier of leg and foot. All that library time, perhaps, or chill winter nights cooped up in Cambridge.

One day, they will take their revenge with six-figure starting salaries and, eventually, sprawling country estates. For now, the Harvard women are taking a drubbing. Not a match do they win.

"Can we go now, Dad?" one of the kids asks, uncomfortable with this slaughter.

"Sure," I say.

On the way back to the motel, we split up. The rest of the family heads off shopping. I head off to do more research. That's right: I'm checking out bars.

Any good father would check out the bars surrounding a prospective college. Are they safe? Are the parking lots well-lighted? On "The Sopranos," Tony takes his daughter on a college tour and disappears one afternoon to "whack" some mob rat. Me, I just go off to have a beer.

ASU may be a dry campus, but a block or two away you can manage to find a cold beverage. I wander into a place that is quiet and dark on a Monday afternoon. For a moment, I think I may have stumbled upon the ASU library.

"What can I get you?" the young bartender/librarian asks.

"I'll have a beer," I say.

"What kind?"

"Surprise me," I say, because that's how you talk in a bar, like a wise guy about to get whacked.

I sit in the bar nursing my beer and having flashbacks. It's been more than 20 years since I sat in a college bar on a Monday afternoon.

Back then, tuition was low. Streaking was popular. Love was free, or at least affordable.

Back then, everyone on a college campus was pretty much naked all the time, except for some of the more conservative sororities, the Delta Gamma house, for one.

Fortunately, college bars have not changed much. On the fat wooden bar rail, students have scratched dirty sonnets with Bic pens. Along the wall, there are dartboards, game tables. A mighty jukebox.

Stale beer and disinfectant fill the air – good smells, the scents of fun and vigorous hygiene.

"Just visiting?" the bartender asks.

"Actually, I'm your dean," I say.

"Nice to meet you," he says.

"Nice to meet you, too," I say.

"Another one?" he says, eyeing my empty glass.

"Why not?"

March 7, 2001

◆ ◆ ◆

Christmas at Our House

HERE we go again. We're not sure where my lovely and patient older father went. First, he takes his Christmas nap, like he always does Christmas Day around 2 p.m. Then he gets up and starts going through all the Christmas cards we received, studying them close up, like he does his hairline in the mirror. The next thing we know he's going out the door.

"Where you going, Dad?" someone asks.

"To the store," he says.

And my mom asks him, what do we need so badly that he has to go out on Christmas Day, and he says lottery tickets and Bloody Mary mix, and she says why can't he spend the whole day with his family like other fathers, and he says, "Because we're out of Bloody Mary mix."

And that's when he left. Like that. Up the chimney he rose.

"Should I call the cops?" I ask Mom after about an hour.

"Let's wait a little longer," Mom says.

"How long?"

"About a month," she says, then tells me to go ahead and finish his column, on account of it doesn't look like he will and we need the cash.

Let's see, where should I start? Did I tell you I'm his daughter? The oldest one. I told you, right?

You know, there's lots of stuff that goes on around here he doesn't even tell you about. Like how he has a Bloody Mary every Christmas, just one or two on account of he says the holidays and alcohol don't mix, though him and Mom seem pretty giggly lately for no apparent reason.

They go a whole year without drinking hardly anything but beer and wine and an occasional margarita, then Christmas comes and he starts drinking Bloody Marys.

He says it's because his knees and joints hurt from being down on the floor doing all the gift-wrapping and stuff. Says the Bloody Marys ease the pain.

"It's medicinal," he keeps saying.

"Of course it is," my mom says, like she's some kind of pharmacist.

"Besides, I like celery," he says.

Mom says my Dad's turning into Arthur Godfrey on account of he's started wearing these baggy old sweaters and slippers, even in public, and that instead of a ukulele he carries a Bloody Mary.

She might be right. I never heard of Arthur Godfrey, let alone a ukulele, which I guess is some kind of a drink. Thank God for spellcheck, that's all I can say.

Other than that, we've had a pretty good Christmas. On Christmas Eve, Dad made this giant pot of chili like he always does on Christmas Eve.

There was so much garlic that I swear the trees in the frontyard died from all the garlic smell.

"Dad, close the front window!" I finally yelled at him.

"Why?" he asked.

"Because you're killing nature," I said.

Then we go to church, which is always an experience, us in church.

Once, when my little brother was way younger, we went to this Christmas Eve service in this pretty little church where we used to live, New Orleans or someplace.

And there we were, sitting in this nice church that we didn't even belong to, admiring all the candles, and my baby brother looks at the candles and says, real loud, "Happy Birthday, Mommy!" like that, so that everyone in the church hears.

Fortunately, they all laughed. Now when we go to church, I usually sit in the back by myself.

So this year we go to church, then we come home and Dad won't let us turn on the television or e-mail our friends or anything on account of he says it's Christmas Eve and we need a little family time. Great. That's just what I need at Christmas. More family time.

Whatever.

Then he and Mom sit on the couch and talk about what it was like when we were real little and how wonderful it was. Then they start getting all gooey on the couch, like two giant chocolate chip cookies mating.

"What do you want for Christmas, really?" my mom asks him.

"How's about a sponge bath?" my dad says.

"That's what I gave you last Christmas," she says.

"I know," my dad says.

Yew!!! How gross is that? Yew!!! Like, I'm supposed to ever want to get married or middle-aged after hearing stuff like that. Yew!!!

After that, we all went to bed, except for Mom and Dad, who stayed up and dragged stuff out of every nook and cranny of the house, "trying to get the house ready for Santa Claus," they told my little sister, and she believed it.

Then they went to bed, and seems like five minutes later it's 7 a.m. already and the whole place is up and someone's making coffee real loud and the phone is ringing from the East Coast.

I'm, like, can't we do this later? I'm a teenager. I can't get up at 7 a.m. I'm lucky to be up by noon.

It's so disgusting how much stuff there is for Christmas at our house. They are like Christmas maniacs. Mom makes us keep lists of who we got stuff from, like, is that sweater from Grandma and is that CD from Uncle Jack? As if anybody even listens to No Doubt anymore. But we have to keep track of it all anyway.

By this time, my brother, he's got pieces of Scotch tape all over his socks and in his hair, and my dad makes a fire in the fireplace with all the old boxes and wrapping paper, which isn't exactly something you want to watch when he has his robe on.

Then we clean up and Dad takes his traditional Christmas nap, on account of he gets real tired seeing how much money Mom spent and he needs to go dream of when he was single and broke as opposed to married and broke, the way he is now. I guess his whole life, he's been broke. Like that dude Bob Cratchit.

Anyway, I guess that's why he's off buying Bloody Mary mix right this minute and playing the lottery. I guess when you get to be his age, all you need is a little hope. A little hope and a little Bloody Mary mix.

Look at the bright side. At least he's not making any more of that chili. Did I tell you about all the garlic he used? I swear, the paint was peeling.

December 27, 2000

◆ ◆ ◆

Taking the Firstborn to College

YOU hear stories about this, how kids grow up and you have to cart them off to college. You think it won't happen to you.

"I'm too young," you think. "There's plenty of time."

But then it happens. Toddlers become teenagers. Teenagers become college kids. No, that's not a knife twisting in your ever-growing gut. It's just one of your kids leaving home, that's all.

"I'm putting some good music on now," my lovely and patient older daughter says as we zoom along the interstate.

Let's begin, as John Cheever liked to, at the beginning. We're on this bittersweet road trip to college. A father and daughter driving down the interstate and growing closer just as we're about to go our separate ways.

"Who's this?" I ask as she pushes a new CD into the player.

"This is Train," she says.

"John Coltrane?"

"No, Train," she says.

> Now that she's back in the atmosphere
> With drops of Jupiter in her hair, hey, hey
> She acts like summer and walks like rain
> Reminds me that there's time to change, hey, hey.

OK, so it's not Cole Porter. Dylan, either. But it's not so bad. Better than rap. Your dog's intestinal noises are better than rap.

In fact, the song by Train is kind of catchy. After a few strains, my older daughter begins to sing along.

> Tell me, did you fall for a shooting star
> One without a permanent scar
> And did you miss me while you were looking for yourself out there.

I'm sure there are many things we will miss about each other, my daughter and I. She'll miss my snoring from two rooms away and the way I burn pork chops on the grill.

Me? I'll miss the way she clears her throat before she answers the phone. Her late-night laugh. Her efforts to make me into a better parent. Everything. I may even miss her messy room. Think how many times you've complained about your kid's messy room, then actually ended up missing the mess when she went off to college. Not me. Not one bit.

"You know, I don't think I'm going to miss you that much," I tease.

"Why?"

"Because you sing awful," I tell her.

We drive south down the Golden State Freeway, past the other colleges that her friends are attending – closer colleges, that smell of juniper trees and diesel.

She tells me she was accepted at one of them. A very good school. But she never bothered to tell us.

"Anything else you haven't told me?" I ask.

"In my whole life or just about college?"

"Your whole life," I say.

47

"No," she says.

In the trunk and back seat, there are 300 bucks worth of items my daughter doesn't really need. Toilet brushes and can openers. Tupperware containers and cough syrup.

It's not really for her. It's for her mother. Her mother needs to know her little girl has all this stuff, even if she never uses it.

"Look at all those grapes," I say as we head out of Orange County.

Off to the right, there is acre after acre of vineyards. Used to be, subdivisions were what you saw springing up all over the place as you traveled California. Now it's vineyards. Eventually, California will be one long vineyard, from the desert to the sea.

"Sure could go for some grape juice right now," I say.

"Why don't you put in another CD?" my daughter says.

As she drives, I browse her CD collection. There is Weezer and Traffic. But there are also the Beatles and Steve Miller.

"Oh, my God," I say.

"What?"

"Somebody has put real music in your CD case," I say.

"Those are mine," she says.

"Get out," I say.

"Really, Dad," she says.

You think your kid is prepared for college, but you never really know. You've taught her a lot. How to save a buck. How to tie a fish hook. Other stuff too. Little boys pretty much raise themselves. With little girls, your job is never really done.

"Here's what you need to know for college," you tell her.

"Oh, jeesh," she sighs.

"No, listen," you say.

So I give her my 1970s view of how to cope with college. I tell her that in any philosophy or history class, she can ensure at least a C grade by asking: "What about John Stuart Mills' view of free will? Isn't that why all governments ultimately fail?" And in almost any sort of science course, you say, in a world-weary way: "Einstein's theories? Tip of the iceberg."

I explain to her that those two observations got me to where I am now, riding along an interstate with her in a dusty Civic, cursing the prices of every gas station we pass and pining for music from 30 years ago.

"Thanks, Dad," she says. "I'll remember all that."

"Good, because it's a hot, cruel world out there," I say.

"Dad, while I'm gone, could you feed my frog?" she asks.

"Sure," I say.

She's been preparing for college for 10 years now, maybe longer. In the eighth grade, she started packing. By 10th grade, she began to load the car. Now at 18, she's preparing to say goodbye for good. As if there's ever anything good about a goodbye.

"And you can delete my screen name on AOL," she says.

"So you're really going?" I ask.

"Yes, Daddy, I'm really going."

This time, I think she means it.

September 5, 2001

◆ ◆ ◆

Ready or Not, There She Goes

So they arrive, these suburban kids, soft as oatmeal, raised without any real hardships except maybe their overly attentive parents and those cheap ink-jet printers that just won't print.

Into freshman dorms they come, the kind of multi-unit housing only Karl Marx could love.

"Where do I park?" my lovely and patient older daughter asks.

"Over there," I say.

As my daughter pulls into a parking place, she tilts her chin up to see over the hood, just the way her mother does.

"How's that?" my daughter asks.

"Maybe your best ever," I say.

"Let's go," she quickly says.

What's the rush, you ask? College is the rush.

We're on this college campus in San Diego, L.A.'s pampered little suburb to the south. A beautiful campus. An educational Oz.

"Mind if I stay?" I ask my daughter.

"Yes," she says.

OK, so we've gotten that out of the way. I can't stay. But I can nose around a little. Peek inside the library. Sniff the dorms for beer.

"Here, carry this," someone says, handing me a lamp.

"And this, too," they say, piling on some pillows.

The dads are the oxen of a freshman dorm. They pile us high with lamps and rugs and clothing, then point us toward a double door.

By the thousands, these dad-oxen come. When we're done, our children reward us by leaving.

"She doesn't seem too upset," I tell my wife after unloading both cars.

"About what?"

"About leaving home," I say.

What's to be upset about? The campus is terrific. The kids seem pleasant enough as teenagers go, little Holden Caulfields, with cell phones holstered in their saggy cargo pants.

"Look at that guy," I tell my son.

It's a show, seeing what kids bring to college. Most carry their stacks of CDs and their Dell computers.

But one ambitious young scholar is carrying in golf clubs, a surfboard and a guitar.

We spot other surfboards, but this is the only guy with a board, sticks and a guitar.

I guess some kids seize the day. Other kids seize the surf and the first tee. Carpe college, baby.

"He'll be gone in a year," I tell the boy.

"Why?"

"He just will," I say.

Outside the campus bookstore, a couple of kids discuss the current state of campus romance.

"Next time I get into a serious relationship, it's not going to be monogamous," a boy says. "I'm sick of that."

"You can't limit yourself," a young woman says. "You have to go for it."

"Exactly," the boy says.

At the campus center, three other young scholars discuss sports and current events.

"The football game starts at 7," one kid says. "So we'll probably start boozin' about 4."

Of course, these days that sort of stuff only takes place off campus. Most college campuses are pretty much dry now.

Back in the 1970s, when the drinking age was still 12, beer was everywhere. At floor parties, pep rallies. Breakfast.

Not anymore. Today, there's not a keg in sight. Like love beads and the SDS, a thing of the past.

Leave it to us parents, once the most blasted generation of college students ever, to impose this new Prohibition on our children. Leave it to us to take the high out of higher education.

"OPEN BAR, 18 AND UP," screams an ad in the student newspaper about some Tijuana saloon 20 miles to the south.

"That's great," I tell my wife as I read the ad. "We're driving them out of the country."

"I've already talked to her about all that Tijuana stuff," she says.

"Good," I say, meaning every word.

Back in the dorm room, the last boxes are emptied. My daughter stacks photos of her high school friends along her desk.

It's a new dorm, though like all freshmen dorms, it'll soon be a breeding ground for mononucleosis and bad political debate.

Once the moms and dads leave, they'll probably sit around, these Holden and Holly Caulfields, sit around these dorms late at night with their cell phones and their pierced navels and question their parents' values. Until one day they'll miss the comfort of it all and pursue the good life, too, while gradually growing up to become their parents.

It's a sad cycle in some ways, but reassuring in others. Sort of funny-ironic. Eventually, everything in life becomes funny-ironic.

"Maybe, as they settle into their new lives, they'll learn to be a little more respectful and appreciative of all these things," one of the roommates' dads suggests as we sit around watching our girls unpack.

I kind of doubt it. Then again, at college almost anything is possible.

"We should go," my wife finally says.

"Not yet," says the little girl.

"Yeah, we should go," I say.

There are hugs and last-minute advice.

"Don't forget to, you know, shower," her mother says.

"After you sneeze," her little sister advises, "you should wash your hands for as long as it takes to sing 'Happy Birthday.' "

"Thanks," says her big sister, hugging her the hardest.

I stand there, taking small breaths, while my wife fluffs our daughter's pillow for the last time.

She fluffs it, smacks it square, fluffs it some more, just like she's been doing nightly for 18 years.

"There," my wife finally says.

"Nice work," I say.

"There," she says again, fluffing it some more.

More quick hugs, all around. Someone swallows hard. Maybe it was me.

Then, suddenly, there are just the four of us, back in the car, back on the busy highway home.

Thank God for our kids. Thank God for freshman dorms, the last playground we'll ever take them to.

Good luck, baby. Carpe college.

September 12, 2001

Hi, Daddy. College Is Great. Please Send Money.

E–MAILS between a college girl and her dad, autumn 2001:

Hi, Daddy,

Last night I went to my first frat party. It was totally fun. Apparently, at the frats, they don't have all the stupid rules like they do here in the dorms. You wouldn't believe all the crazy stuff they do.

Did they have fraternities when you were in college? Did you ever stay up dancing till 2 a.m.? Just asking. Frankly, Dad, you don't really seem the type.

Please send money.

Hi, honey,

There is winter in the windows and a fire in the fireplace. Your mother and I would be warmed to hear about other things besides fraternity parties. You, for example. Are you eating well? How are your classes? Have you changed your bed sheets?

Hi, Daddy,

Freshman year is unbelievably busy. First, you go to class. Then you sleep a little. Then you go to another class. Then you sleep a little more. With all the naps, it's sort of like kindergarten, except nobody dresses you and combs your hair and stuff.

Speaking of hair, tonight I helped my roommate dye her hair. I really like my roommates. Did I tell you that I drove one of them to get a tattoo? Just a little rose, right on her ankle. It looks so cool. One of these days, I think I'm going to get a tattoo.

Unless you send money.

Hi, honey,

That's good news about your roommates. Are there any other activities at your college besides playing beauty parlor and acquiring tattoos?

Are there books there, for example? Have you found the library? They do have libraries there, right, at that big overbuilt state campus?

If not, you should tell someone in charge that your father suggests they build a library right away.

"Dean Werner," you should say, "my taxpayer-father insists that you build a nice library here first thing in the morning."

Let me know his response.

Hi, Daddy,

Wow. Did you know they have a bowling alley right on campus? Last night, we all watched "Friends," then went bowling together. It was so much fun. On the way back, we found this great place that makes cheesesteak sandwiches, just like in Philadelphia. The juice ran all the way down my elbows. At college, nobody worries too much about manners and stuff. I don't think I've seen a napkin since I've been here.

Don't forget that money.

Hi, honey,

Have you asked about that library yet? I fear that, though fraternities and bowling alleys are excellent places to study and learn, without a library you will grow up to be one of those people who is chronically late, who never uses a turn signal, who confuses Byron with Keats.

That's not the sort of person your mother and I hoped to raise, young lady.

Hi, Daddy,

Did I mention they have concerts here all the time? Blink-182. Dylan. Is the money in the mail?

How's Mom?

Hi, honey,

Your dear mother really misses you. She stays up late worrying that you are OK, as do we all, except of course your little brother, who just noticed you no longer live here.

I'm worried about your mother. The other morning, she told your little sister, "Get dressed now, young lady, or you're going to have to dress yourself." "Huh, Mom?" your little sister said.

Those are the types of conversations you probably miss the most.

Please send money.

No, Daddy,

You're supposed to send me money, remember? Money, money, money. Small bills, mostly 50s.

Hi, honey,

I was disturbed to learn last night that your mother gave you all the leftover manicotti the last time you visited and that you returned with it to school.

As you know, I love leftover manicotti almost as much as life itself and hope you will return some of it. This is fairly urgent, in that I believe I am suffering some sort of midlife crisis that only your mother's manicotti can cure.

Dear Daddy,

 The manicotti is totally gone. So's my money. Please send it now or I am dropping out and coming home to live with you and Mom. Forever.

 Don't you remember what that was like?

Hi, honey,

 Your room awaits you. It's just the way you left it: messy and smelling of nail polish and soccer socks.

 There's a fire in the fireplace. We'll leave a light on.

 Love always, Dad.

November 7, 2001

CHAPTER THREE

THE BOY

◆ ◆ ◆

Reading With Dad

THE boy reads the paragraph, then stops. He likes this paragraph. To him, it is rich with truth, almost profound. He reads it again.

> *People have been trying to understand dogs ever since the beginning of time. One never knows what they'll do. You can read every day where a dog saved the life of a drowning child, or lay down his life for his master.*
>
> *Some people call this loyalty. I don't. I may be wrong, but I call it love – the deepest kind of love.*

"That's true, isn't it, Dad?" the boy says after reading it the second time. "This stuff about dogs."

I nod, and we read aloud some more, first him, then me, sharing this book page by page, chapter by chapter, front to back.

"You really like books, don't you, Dad?" he asks as we pause between chapters.

"They're all right," I say.

Truth is, I like books the way I like cold, foamy drinks in the summer and baseball in the fall. Basically, I live for them.

And now the boy is discovering books too. Almost by accident, the 12-year-old is finding enjoyment in the simple act of reading, a kind of intimacy there is no real expression for.

"Know what 'camaraderie' is?" I ask him at one point.

"Like being friends?" he says.

"Like being pals," I say. "You've become pals with your books."

"Sorry, Dad. I don't get you."

"That's all right," I say. "Just keep reading."

Six months ago, he was indifferent to books. He read only when he had to. And even then, not always.

Six months ago, if someone had offered a magic potion to make him love to read, I would've paid a fortune for it. Even though I don't have a fortune, I would've paid one, borrowing the fortune at 15% interest and paying it back in huge installments over 60 years.

Back then, he thought books were for dorks, prematurely mature boys who couldn't hit a fastball or snag a line drive. Books were for indoor people, people who shunned sunlight and all the other good things in life.

Then, one day, the boy flopped down on the couch and didn't flop back up again.

"Mono?" I asked the doctor.

"Mono," the doctor said.

It was just the bad break he needed. Mono. And for two weeks, he became what he'd always despised – an indoor person.

The mono made him so sleepy, he couldn't watch TV. It left him so weak, he couldn't lift a book.

So I began to read to him. Like when he was 4, I would read to him, hamming it up and trying to bring the words to life.

As he got stronger, we would alternate reading pages aloud, first him, then me. Then, with time, we would alternate chapters. And when he finally recovered, we still alternated chapters.

Now every night before bed, he grabs some book and calls to me. And together we read, elbow to elbow, page by page.

"Dad, you listening?" he'll say.

"Huh?"

"Your turn to read."

"OK," I say, shaking myself awake. And we read some more.

He likes adventure stories mostly. "Old Yeller." "Where the Red Fern Grows." "Hatchet." Stories about boys lost in the woods with only their dogs and their hunting rifles. Stories he gobbles up like movie-house popcorn.

And now this love for reading has gotten so out of hand, he'll even read a daily newspaper, starting with the sports section and working his way forward, the way his dad does.

He reads the Sports section the way people read the wills of rich relatives, scouring the fine print, then rereading the parts he doesn't fully understand.

Mostly, he likes the obscure facts, the stuff he thinks only he will discover.

"Mondesi is only hitting .194," the boy says in disbelief. ".194!"

Each morning, he leans down close to the page, getting his elbows in the newsprint, crinkling the page as he shoves closer to the breakfast table.

The smaller the print, the closer he gets. The smaller the print, the more he cherishes the information.

"Catfish Hunter threw five no-hitters in high school," he says, reading some factoid deep inside sports. "Five no-hitters!"

He stores up these facts for later use, balling them up in his brain like pieces of string, ready to call on them at just the right time, during playground discussions or dugout debates.

"The All-Star game is July 7," he says, pointing to a piece of type no thicker than an eyelash. "July 7 at Coors Field."

There's a pause as he hunts for more factoids, more of the trivia that makes a boy a boy, or a man a man. Or, maybe best of all, a little of both.

"Dad, you listening?" he finally says, both our noses buried in the morning paper.

"Huh?"

"You listening, Dad?"

"Always," I say.

April 22, 1998

◆ ◆ ◆

A Winning Night at Wrigley Field

So here we are in Wrigley Field, one of baseball's finer sanitariums, on an August night with the Cubs in last place and nearly 40,000 fans in the stands, all holding bratwurst and beer.

"Hey, Sammy, how many outs?" someone screams to Sammy Sosa, who holds up one finger from his post in the outfield, as if testing the wind.

"That's right, Sammy!" the fan yells. "One out."

We are in the bleachers, the boy and I, his glove by his side, two regulation National League baseballs nestled inside like quail eggs. Every minute or two, he glances down to make sure the baseballs are still there.

"How they doing?" I ask him.

"Good," he says proudly. "They're doing pretty good."

The boy and I arrived two hours early for the game, snagged a couple of baseballs during batting practice, then sat back to watch the lights come on and the bleachers fill with some of baseball's best fans.

"I'm never washing this shirt," the boy says when ketchup spills from his hot dog.

"I'm never washing these pants," he says an inning later, when he gets mustard on his knee.

I didn't prepare him much for his first visit to Wrigley, didn't burden him in advance with the history or tradition of the place. But after a couple of innings, I can't hold off any longer.

"Your grandfather used to watch games here as a kid," I say.

"He did?" the boy asks.

"And your great-grandfather too," I say.

"Really?" he says.

"Ever see that picture of Babe Ruth pointing to the outfield?" I say. "Happened here."

"I know, Dad," he says, so I stop the history lesson and concentrate on my beer.

Next to us, a vendor appears, his neck bent, his shoulders beginning to cave.

"Peanuts!" the vendor yells, and a young urban prince in a $40 T-shirt pulls out three bucks and tells the vendor to keep the change.

"See that?" I tell the boy.

"What?"

"He tipped the peanut vendor," I say.

"So?" the boy says.

"These bleachers, they've gone downhill," I tell the boy.

Used to be, the bleachers attracted a working-class crowd, sewer workers, bartenders, cops, even the hard-core unemployed. Guys named Mike and Fred and Ziggy. They called themselves the Bleacher Bums. They were interesting to be around.

Now, especially at the night games, the bleachers attract a lot of riffraff: young lawyers, commodities traders, stockbrokers – the sheen of entitlement on their 25-year-old faces, pretty women on their arms, cell phones going off in their pockets before they even manage to sit down.

"We're in the third row," a young Gatsby yells into a cell phone. "Near Aisle 146. No wait, Aisle 147. I don't know, we're near the aisle."

Next to him, his girlfriend slumps, looking bored in the bleachers. Maybe in her mind, there are better places to be.

"We're near the aisle," Gatsby says into the phone during the national anthem.

Behind us, a guy discusses his wedding. Off to the right, a frat boy buys a bratwurst. Beer and brats, the opiate of the upper Midwest.

"Keep the change," he tells the vendor.

Evidently, the city of Chicago has hit the lottery, extra money everywhere, with old neighborhoods being renovated and huge houses – big as airports – going up in the far suburbs.

Now this affluence has even spread to the Wrigley Field bleachers, which attracts an educated, well-bred crowd. A nice crowd, polite and fresh scrubbed. How they got into this place, I'll never know.

"Hey, Chad!" someone yells to a friend, and three guys in polo shirts turn around.

In the fifth inning, with the Cubs down by six runs, it begins to rain, big teardrops for another lost Chicago season. Below us, one of the young urban princes raises an umbrella.

"See that?" I tell the boy.

"What?"

"An umbrella in the bleachers," I tell him.

"What's wrong with that?"

"It's bad manners," I say. "In the old days, you'd never use an umbrella."

Then, like a rainbow, something sort of magic happens. A fan sitting behind the umbrella begins to pour his beer over the umbrella, so that the beer leaks down into the lap of the guy holding the umbrella.

The crowd cheers. The guy with the wet lap closes the umbrella.

"You see that, Dad?" the boy asks.

"Yeah, I saw it," I say with a smile.

In the sixth inning, the rain continues. It falls pretty steadily. Cell phones get wet. Yet no one leaves. The Cubs look awful. Yet no one leaves. At Wrigley, maybe the best things never change.

"Hey, Sammy, make it stop raining!" someone yells.

Beside me, a young suburban prince soaks up the game and another hot dog. At his side, two batting practice baseballs, safe and warm in his well-oiled glove.

"I'm never washing this hand," the boy says, sucking ketchup from a knuckle. "I'm never, ever washing this hand."

August 18, 1999

◆ ◆ ◆

Play Ball, Baby

THE boy is standing in the batting cage, crushing baseballs and singing a Sinatra song.

"You make me feel so young. . . ."

Thwack!

"You make me feel there are songs to be sung. . . ."

Thwack!

The rest of the country is still chipping ice off the sidewalks, and here we are at the batting cage on a recent sunny day, hitting baseballs and feeling young, saluting spring in early February.

"You make me feel so young," sings the boy, ripping another line drive.

Even without a big orchestra behind him, the boy sounds good. He is using his voice like a slide trombone, the way Sinatra used to. It's a little high, this voice. But it's still Sinatra, the Chairman of the Board, three octaves up.

"You make me feel like spring has sprung. . . ."

Thwack!

The boy only knows the one Sinatra song. He heard it on the stereo recently, and he just can't get it out of his head. Not the song so much. It's the voice he keeps hearing. That Sinatra voice. Tough. Confident. Kind of cocky. All the things Frank Sinatra and 12-year-old boys are famous for.

Now the boy sings Sinatra everywhere he goes. In the shower. At the dinner table. Even here, at the batting cage.

"Hey, Dad, I wonder if Sinatra played baseball?" the boy asks.

"Probably," I say.

"I'll bet you're right," he says. "I'll bet Sinatra played center field."

As always, the boy and I go over a lot of stuff here at the batting cage. Important stuff. Like how he should keep his head still when he swings. Or how he got jalapeño juice in his eye last week at lunch and thought he was going to die. Or how the Clippers are just five players away from contending.

When we're done with all that, we talk more about Sinatra.

"Ever hear of the Rat Pack?" I ask him.

"The what?"

"The Rat Pack," I say.

"Don't think so," he says, chopping a grounder back to the pitching machine.

So I tell him about the Rat Pack, about how Sinatra and his buddies hung out together and called everybody "baby" and acted a little like jerks. And how the American public loved them anyway because the Rat Pack was having so much fun.

Back then, you could have a little fun without feeling real guilty about it. Fun didn't carry the stigma it does today. In fact, back then, life was mostly fun.

"Everybody wanted to be in the Rat Pack," I tell the boy.

"You think I would've been in the Rat Pack?" he asks.

"You might've made it," I say. "Hard to tell."

I explain to him that if he had been in the Rat Pack, he would've had to wear a black tuxedo. The Rat Pack loved black tuxedos, with their bow ties sort of tilted and coming off, probably from having so much fun.

"The Rat Pack always wore black tuxes," I say.

"Even when they went swimming?" he asks.

"Especially then," I say.

There's a sparkle in his eye as he hears more about the Rat Pack. He especially likes the stuff about life being mostly fun. He's always been a strong proponent of fun.

And now he's hearing about this group of guys – these adults even – who became famous just for having fun. It gives the boy hope for the future.

"I wish I could've played baseball with the Rat Pack," the boy says.

He imagines what that would've been like, playing baseball all day, then wearing tuxedos with crooked bow ties all night, calling everybody "baby" and making pretty girls laugh. It fits nicely with his concept of the perfect life, a concept he first developed about five minutes ago.

"Hey, baby," he says to his mom when he gets home.

"Hey, who?" his mom asks, not exactly amused.

His mother doesn't really care who calls her baby, as long as it's not her son.

"Why'd he call me 'baby'?" she says, turning toward me as if I automatically had something to do with it.

"He's being a Rat Packer," I tell her.

"A what?"

"I told him about the Rat Pack," I explain.

"Oh, great. Which one are you?" she asks the boy. "Dino?"

"I'm Frankie," he says, with a wink, heading off toward his room with his bat on his shoulder, singing as he goes.

"You make me feel so young. . . ."

February 4, 1998

◆ ◆ ◆

How to Putter

So here we are on this Sunday afternoon, replacing a doorknob on the backdoor.

"Screwdriver," I say.

"Phillips or flat?" asks the boy.

"Flat."

I am teaching the boy how to putter around. He is 11 now, and it's never too early for a kid to learn how to putter around the house with Dad, doing stuff but not really doing stuff, all the while appearing to actually be doing stuff.

"So it's like homework," he says.

"No," I explain. "Homework is serious. Puttering is purely recreational."

"OK," he says.

He watches me put the flange on the door handle, taking time to line it up just right, measuring twice, then marking it carefully with my carpenter's pencil.

I am taking this opportunity to show him how to do a job really well. One simple task done absolutely right. It is the first small step on the road to excellence.

"Ouch," I say.

"Screwdriver slip?" he asks.

"Yep."

"Ouch," he says sympathetically.

He watches me struggle with the door handle awhile longer. He sees me study it closely and examine it from all sides, trying to anticipate any problems, the way real craftsmen do.

"You stick your tongue out when you work," he says. "Like Michael Jordan."

I like that he thinks I'm like Michael Jordan. Somehow, I don't get compared to Jordan often enough.

"You really look silly with your tongue out, Dad," he says.

So I decide to let him tighten the flange himself. Right away, I notice that he doesn't stick his tongue out when he works. This is a bad sign. Sticking your tongue out gives you extra powers of concentration.

But he seems to do OK anyway. He tightens the last screw, then belches proudly.

"Sorry," he says with a laugh.

"I can fix that, you know."

"Fix what?"

"That belch," I say, grabbing a pair of pliers. "Come here."

I grab him and wrestle him to the floor, pretending that I am going to remove his belch, which is located somewhere near the tonsils or inside the esophagus.

"Quit laughing!" I order, as I pin him to the floor. "This procedure is difficult enough!"

That's when his mother enters the room. She walks in like a woman who has just walked in on a burglary, taking two steps forward, then three steps back, clearly alarmed by what she is seeing.

"What are you two doing?" she asks.

"We're putzing around," the boy says.

"Puttering," I whisper.

"Right. We're puttering around," the boy says.

"Oh wonderful," she says.

We can tell from the way she says "oh wonderful" that what she really means is, "Lord help me." Or, "Someone call an attorney."

It wasn't so long ago that she liked it when her husband did chores. When we were first married, I would renovate a bathroom or re-pipe a kitchen almost overnight, while she flitted around like Audrey Hepburn, arranging flowers and being all chirpy, sometimes breaking into the theme from "Camelot" for no reason at all. Because that's how life looked, full of renovation. Full of hope.

Then the kids came along and my renovation efforts grew less intense. No remodeling. No re-piping. Instead, there were soccer games and birthday parties.

That left time for a doorknob here and a leaky faucet there, but never much more. Occasionally, she'd find me in the basement workshop, asleep in my old recliner as the Dodger game played on the radio, gathering strength for my next chore.

And today, she finds that I am teaching her son the same sort of work habits, how to stretch one small task into an afternoon of simple pleasures.

"Oh wonderful," she says again, her shoulders sagging.

Now, instead of Audrey Hepburn, she is like some Kennedy wives, her spirit broken, her sense of humor crushed, knowing that there is no hope for the kitchen ever getting remodeled or the house painted.

"I have a little list," she says, handing us a tiny slip of paper.

She keeps handing me lists because she knows she can never give up. To give up on the chores would be to surrender to the idea that nothing will ever get done.

"Just don't overdo it," she says with a smirk.

The boy and I look at the list of chores. The list is on a small slip of paper no bigger than a cash register receipt. But it is packed with writing. Tiny writing, maybe 100 lines long.

"What's this, Dad?"

"It's our little list," I say.

We huddle over it as if gazing at a court summons.

Drippy sink.

Sticky garage door.

Leaky roof.

"Everything ends with 'y,' " the boy says.

He's right. Drippy. Sticky. Leaky. Yucky. It's like a roster of the lost dwarfs. And to a home-repair beginner, a list like this can seem overwhelming.

"We're supposed to do all this today?" the boy asks. "Or is it, like, all the chores for our entire lives?"

I take the list and study it closely.

I explain that the secret to puttering is to never pick something that can't be finished in an hour or two. Which leaves plenty of time for other activities, like listening to a ballgame or visiting the hardware store, which is the very best part of puttering around.

"Come on," I say. "We need to get a key made."

"Which one?" he asks.

"Doesn't matter."

So we head off toward the car, two guys on a Sunday afternoon mission, walking one after the other, the way guys do, not side by side, because that would imply equality. And frankly, guys aren't all that keen on equality. They prefer a leader, a person clearly in charge. It gives them somebody to ridicule.

"We're just ducking out, aren't we, Dad?" the boy says, picking up this puttering-around stuff pretty quickly.

"Ducking out?" I say. "No way. We've got lots of stuff to do. A whole list of stuff."

"OK, Dad," he says, smiling. "I'm right behind you."

August 5, 1997

Heading for the Rapids

"I think I'm going to law school."

"You are?"

And I might, at that. I explain that I know some bad lawyers but no poor ones. They all seem to have boats or mountain homes. I need a profession where you succeed even if you fail.

"You don't wanna go to law school," my friend Bob says.

"There's already too many lawyers," says my buddy Bill.

They might be right. There are three of them on this father-son rafting trip. You can tell them apart right away. When the lawyers fall in the river, the fish jump out.

There's also a dealership operations manager, a minister and me, a writer of no renown. When I fall in the river, the lawyers jump out.

Our sons are here, too. All told, a baker's dozen of outdoor enthusiasts, deep in the Sequoia National Forest, a mere four hours from L.A.'s hyper heartbeat.

Cell phones can't beep here. Pagers lose their buzz. The worst insects of modern life, all dead.

"You just head down that path till you reach the water," one of the guides says as we pile off the rafting company's bus.

"How far?"

"Three miles," the guide says.

Three miles that feel like six. We have backpacks, each loaded with 30 pounds of gear and clothing. One guy is wearing a Scooby-Doo Band-Aid on his big toe. We are nothing if not prepared.

"How'd you hurt your toe?" someone asks.

"Basketball," I say. "Kid pushed me into the flower bed."

"Sounds like a foul," the guy says.

"Definitely," I say.

We trudge down the path, hearing whitewater in the distance. We round a bend only to find another bend. Six dads more accustomed to leather office chairs and golf carts.

Our sons, meanwhile, glide easily down the trail. Like mimes, they walk funny on purpose. The last hundred yards, one of them actually runs.

"That's so disgusting," one of the dads says.

It's a three-day raft trip, and we've started it well, the fathers sweating off 5 pounds each while hiking to our launch point. At the river's edge, we mill around as if looking for a sofa.

"Can't wait for the rapids," one of them says, then plops down on a log.

And what rapids these are. The Forks of the Kern is considered one of the finer river runs anywhere, because the rapids line up one after another, white as your mother's wedding dress.

Beneath the whitewater? Granite boulders, large and larger. Wedge your foot beneath one of these monsters and the Kern River will slam you to its floor. You'll come up for air maybe never.

Conk your head. Fracture a collarbone. Burst an aorta. No 911 here. It's just you and God and a $4 plastic paddle.

"You're in the wilderness, a long way from help," a guide warns.

"Now they tell me," I mutter, looking at my Scooby-Doo Band-Aid.

"OK, let's get into the rafts," the guide says.

In our raft, there's the boy and me, plus a lawyer named Rocky and his son, Nick.

I am hoping for the minister, but instead I get a guy named Rocky, down a lethal stretch of whitewater. Irony: I wear it like a shroud.

"Did I mention I'm going to law school?" I ask.

"If you survive," Rocky says.

And off we go on our trip. Six boats, six guides and our tender platoon of fathers and sons.

The guides are the sort of men we thought we'd all grow up to be. Tough as two-by-fours. Good with knots and snake bites. Bar maids, too, probably.

In the summer, they guide raft trips. In the winter, they work the ski runs of Tahoe or Mammoth.

"I live like a millionaire," one of them says. "I just have no money."

For three days we all live like millionaires. The best whitewater rafting is as exhilarating as deep-sea fishing but far more dangerous – exhausting and refreshing all at once.

"Next up, Needlerock Falls," our guide says. "OK, boys, put your game faces on."

Class IV and V rapids, almost all. Basically, the rating system works like this: If it thrashes like a Maytag, it's a Class IV. If it thrashes like a Maytag that could kill you, it's a Class V. Simple, really.

"Once, an oar boat went off this one and folded in two," one of the guides explains about Vortex, a Class V rapid with a 10-foot plunge. "It never came up."

We paddle hard through even the most dangerous stretches, the torque of the oars holding us tight to the river.

It seems the most counterintuitive thing, reaching out of the raft with a paddle as the boat ricochets between rocks and hissing rapids. Takes half a day just to get used to it.

"Keep paddling!" our guide orders over and over. "Dig!"

At night, we camp along the river. The dads slurp foamy beer and rub their tired arms while the boys fish for rainbow trout. The guides cook. A full moon peeks up over the granite canyon wall, watching.

Here's what the dads talk about: EBay. Interest rates. Bush's chances for a second term. America's corporate creeps.

As the river roars past, we talk about California's water wars. "Chinatown" and the great book "Cadillac Desert."

We talk about ski boats and Little League controversies and how parents ruin youth sports.

We talk about "Caddyshack" and "Animal House" and the demise of drive-in theaters. Classic television, too.

"The Golden Age of TV?" says Bill. " 'The Beverly Hillbillies' ?"

"I've got a theory on that," Rocky says.

"Huh?"

" 'The Beverly Hillbillies' represented America's transformation from an agrarian economy to an urban one," explains Rocky

"It did?"

"Jed Clampett was the Jeffersonian ideal of the yeoman farmer," he says. "Elly May was Diana the Huntress."

"I caught a fish!" yells the boy.

"You did?"

The sounds of a bunch of guys out in the wilderness, 50 miles from the nearest freeway. The campfire sizzles. One dad belches. Another does something even less eloquent.

" 'Blazing Saddles,' now that was a great movie," someone notes.

Twenty guys, finally away from the false comforts of modern life.

Twenty guys out in the woods, living like millionaires.

July 3, 2002

◆ ◆ ◆

At Last, the Waterfall

WHEN we last met, the Kern River was threatening to swallow us like hors d'oeuvres, and a couple of the dads were talking about the cultural significance of "The Beverly Hillbillies" and making plans to have a well-chilled beer at the end of the raft trip.

"Jethro Bodine is the primary comic character," my friend Rocky is saying. "Because what does Jethro want to be? A double-aught spy. But he betrays himself as the yeoman farmer."

"And Granny is still fighting the Civil War," my friend Bill adds.

"Exactly."

You meet a lot of crazies out here in the woods. Often, they're your closest friends.

Then there's this British guy, one of the guides, who leads us coolly through stretches of rock and water like someone shooting 18 holes. Churchill is his name. Dave Churchill. Wears a helmet decorated with the British flag, because most folks assume he's Australian.

"Nice work, mates!" Churchill says after we pinball through a stretch of whitewater.

"What'd he say?"

"We did OK, mate," says the boy.

For three days, we have been working our way down the Forks of the Kern, one of America's finest rafting rivers. We've eaten strawberries and jerky for lunch. Steak for dinner.

Yes, when we last met, we were having a heck of a time, crazies and all. An adventurous trip – bruising but not brutal.

Now along comes Carson Falls.

"This is the big daddy," a guide warns.

"I thought I was the big daddy," my friend Howard says.

"Not anymore," someone says.

Lewis and Clark had the rugged Bitterroot Mountains to contend with. We have Carson Falls.

Our little armada of fathers and sons is itching to try Carson Falls, the final and most difficult hurdle on our 20-mile raft trip. There's three lawyers, a minister, the car guy. If anyone is frightened, he's not talking.

"I can't wait for Carson," the boy keeps saying.

"Me either," I lie.

Not since our honeymoons have the dads faced anything quite this strenuous. We are mostly in our mid-40s. Our foreheads are like camper shells. Our shoulders wide yet soft. We drive decent cars and live in nice homes. When something bad happens in our lives, we call someone to fix it. The roof. The furnace. An aging tooth.

But there's no fixing Carson Falls.

It is crafted of granite, permanently fractured, edges like an ax.

Through it runs the Kern. On the surface, pretty as a petticoat. A swirling caldron below.

"Sure you want to do this?" I ask the boy.

"Sure," he says.

Oh, sure, nothing to fear here. If you survive the 10-foot waterfall, there's a suck hole 20 yards beyond. Hit that wrong, and your wife is out dating again.

Hit it wrong, and the yard won't be mowed for months. The new kitchen will never be painted. At Christmas, your wife puts up the tree herself, cursing you the entire time. How's that for a legacy?

"Mates, the way to run this," Churchill says, "is to stay close to that giant boulder."

We have parked our rafts and are standing on the shore studying Carson

Falls. As we watch, thousands of gallons of snowmelt crash against the rocks. In its spit, rainbows form.

"It's not so bad," the boy finally says, and three grown men laugh.

I look at the boy. He won't look at me now.

"When we hit the falls, I want everyone to get down into the raft and just hold on," Churchill says.

"Stay in the boat," says Rocky. "Like in 'Apocalypse Now.'"

"Nice reference," I mumble. On my right, I have Churchill. On my left, Francis Ford Coppola.

So we pile back in our raft, me and Rocky, our two sons, Churchill.

"I think I'm staying with the boat," I tell the boy.

"Me, too," he says.

And for the first 10 seconds of our voyage, things go incredibly well. Then, even before we reach the waterfall, we bump this little lip of rock that sends Rocky flying out of the raft.

"Get him in the boat!" Churchill yells as we approach the waterfall. "Get him in the boat!"

Big guy, Rocky. Two-hundred-plus pounds of Ivy League lawyer, bobbing like a champagne cork in the churning Kern. When he goes in, the river rises about 3 inches.

"Get him in the boat!" the guide yells.

I know this is serious because Churchill has lost his British accent. For two days, he has sounded like Ringo Starr. Now he's talking American.

"Get him in the #%*&x!# boat!"

Seconds before the waterfall, Rocky's son Nick and I manage to pull Rocky back in the boat. He gasps as if harpooned.

"You OK?"

"Who?"

"Get down!" Churchill yells.

In slow motion, here's what happens next:

We all hit the floor as the raft belly-flops over the falls, which causes my knees to push up into my chin, which causes my central nervous system to completely collapse.

So far, so good.

The raft slams into the water, jiggles like a starlet, then bounces wickedly across the rapids.

"Hold on!" Churchill screams.

Hold on? To what? To Rocky? There's no telling when he'll go flying back in the river. To my son? Yeah, right. There's 30 years of therapy.

"Hold on!" I scream as we tumble down Carson Falls, a pleasant ride if you have the loins for it, but not without an occasional risk.

"Whew!" someone yells when we clear the last rapids.

"Yes!" says the boy.

"Yes!" says Nick.

"Everyone OK?" Churchill asks.

I have a bruise the size of Cincinnati. Rocky looks like he just wrestled Moby-Dick. Sure, we're fine.

And onward down the mighty Kern we go.

July 10, 2002

◆ ◆ ◆

There's Nothing Fair About a Fairway

IT'S a nice sunny day here in South Florida, so we ruin it with golf. Poison it with our putting. Torture ourselves with shots that roar off the tee like the worst sneeze you ever had, slicing so severely that the ball ends up almost behind us, turning a 520-yard par five into a 620-yard par five. That's how our day is going. For a while, it's like we're playing backward.

"Nice shot, Dad," the boy says.

"Thank you," I say.

It is a measure of how much I love this kid that I even attempt this crazy game. He wants to show his grandfather how well he plays, and they invited me along.

"Sure," I lied, "I'd love to play."

And off into the muggy Florida morning we go. Warriors really. Zooming off on our electric horses, me with borrowed clubs and the boy with a used set he received for Christmas. Our tools of torture. Graphite shafts.

"Watch my 7-iron," he says.

"I'm watching," says his grandfather.

The boy is young and naive enough to think that this game can be played for pleasure. Like Tiger on TV, he sends sharp shots off toward the green, believing against all odds that everything will turn out for the best.

"Watch my wedge, Grandpa," he says.

"Check your stance," his grandpa advises.

The boy thinks only of the future, only of the time he will march down the 18th fairway at Augusta and claim the green jacket.

Maybe next year, he thinks. Or the year after. Because golf champions are getting younger and younger all the time. So the future is now. If he waits too long, some hotshot third-grader will come along and dominate the game.

"Hey, what did you have?" I ask as we leave the second green.

"A six," the boy says.

"You sure?" I ask.

"Or a seven maybe," he says.

I'm pretty sure Huck Finn here is shaving strokes. He is also, apparently, giving himself a mulligan on almost every hole.

"Oops," he says after a bad shot, then reaches into his pocket for a second ball, drops it quickly and takes a bonus swipe.

"That's better," he says, before heading down the fairway.

It's like he's playing best ball all by himself. It's OK, because this Florida course is mostly deserted in the late morning. It's a luxury you hardly ever find back home in Southern California.

"I think he's shaving strokes," I tell his grandfather.

"Really?"

"He five-putted," I say.

"He's just polishing his game," his grandfather explains.

Me, I'm polishing my game, too. For every decent shot, I slap three miserable ones. That's one for four. In baseball, I'd be making $2.5 million a year.

"If you worked on it a little, you could be pretty good," my father-in-law says.

"Yeah, maybe," I say.

Truth is, I have worked on it. Like the boy, I started young. But too many double bogeys dragged me down. By age 25, I'd quit the game.

Now I am back. So is my old game. I hit the short and mid irons pretty well, but my long game is a disaster.

"Oh, jeesh," I say with every C-shaped tee shot.

By the fifth hole, it's pretty clear that the devil is in my driver. There are demons in my 3-iron as well. I don't need a golf lesson, I need an exorcist.

Jack Nicklaus needs to show up wearing a priest's collar and waving a crucifix over my woods and long irons.

"Oh mighty God," Father Nicklaus would say. "Save this man from his demons. Save this man from golf."

By the back nine, I begin to set some reasonable goals for this round. One sweet shot. That's all I ask – that one great shot that keeps you coming back.

All it will take is a little patience. And a driver with a sweet spot the size of a schnauzer.

By the 10th hole, the change in my pocket has all melted together in the Florida heat. And my back is stiffening.

On tee shots, I seem able to coil but not uncoil. I look like Red Buttons playing in some sort of special pro-am for people with bad backs.

"Hey, Dad," the boy yells.

"What?"

"You're having fun, aren't you?" the boy says as we trudge to the 17th tee. "Admit it, you're having fun."

Maybe I am. One hundred strokes into this thing, and it's sort of fun. My pocket change has melted. My wallet is laminated to my hip. My back is spaghetti. But I'm having fun, thanks mostly to the fine camaraderie of our little group.

"Hey, Arnie, what'd you have on that last hole?" my father-in-law asks.

"A six," I say.

"I think he's shaving strokes," the father-in-law tells the boy.

"Me, too," the boy says.

The boy pulls his driver from the bag and stares down the 17th fairway. He tugs at his sleeve. He takes a practice swing. Then another. Finally, he lunges at the ball, as if lancing a boil.

The ball sails 150 yards straight down the fairway, a beautiful drive, true as a Sunday sermon.

One great shot.

Just my luck. I ask for one great shot, and God gives it to him.

"Next time, I'm being more specific," I mumble to myself.

"What, Dad?"

"I said 'Nice tee shot,' " I tell him.

"Thanks," the boy says.

August 23, 2000

◆ ◆ ◆

The Joy of Camping

I'M sitting by the campfire, watching my son trying to eat the bratwurst I just cooked for him.

It is so tough, this bratwurst, that he is having trouble tearing off even the smallest bite. And when he finally does, he chews so hard that I can see those little bones along his temples – those little tectonic plates in the side of the head – working overtime against each other.

He does not, bless his little heart, complain about my cooking. He just concentrates on the meal, killing it softly with his little squirrel teeth.

"Not bad," he finally says. "Not bad at all."

This year an estimated 60 million Americans will head out to the wilderness, making camping one of the most popular family-oriented recreational activities.

What makes for a successful trip? I really don't know. And I'm willing to share what I don't know with you right here.

* * *

SETTING UP THE TENT: One measure of a man is how he sets up a rental tent at 9 in the evening, by flashlight, with all the kids watching.

It's not a great measure, just a measure.

The tent comes in a surprisingly tiny box, no bigger than a carton of Velveeta cheese. Wait, this is a carton of Velveeta cheese. Shine that flashlight over here, son.

OK, here's the tent. The instructions, bless their little hearts, are carefully folded and creased so that the most essential information is almost unreadable. For example, the first section reads: "Spread out all the parts on the ground. Now — ."

That's the crease line, all squished into hyphens. As a rule, every 12th line of tent instructions is a crease line.

Against all odds, the tent goes up in 45 minutes. And there are only six or seven leftover parts.

Piece of cake, this camping.

* * *

BUILDING A FIRE: The campfire takes on additional importance because here on the mountain, smack dab in the middle of summer, the temperature is hovering around 40 degrees. As I try to light the fire, the kids huddle around and offer advice.

"Dad, you're going to blow us up," the oldest daughter says.

"Huh?"

"All that lighter fluid," she says. "We're gonna scorch."

Sure enough, the freshly lighted fire makes a sort of nuclear whoosh, sending a ball of fire 20 feet into the air. I look down to find that where I once had leg hair, I now have little kernels of former leg hair.

Fortunately, the kids have moved back about half a mile and their leg hair is unharmed.

Piece of cake, this camping.

* * *

GOING TO SLEEP: The kids, bless their little hearts, just love to end the day by slipping into their warm sleeping bags.

It's the actual sleeping they have problems with because once they are in their bags, the kids' favorite activity is watching the shadows flicker against the side of the tent and imagining all the creepy things that are going on out there that will end in their untimely deaths.

They summon, in their little heads, tidbits from every scary movie and bedtime story they have ever heard and assemble them into a giant fright montage.

Meanwhile, I am working on a major headache. Here, 50 miles from the nearest aspirin bottle, the kids have given me a mental wedgy that you would not believe. Just as I'm about to lose my mind, they finally drift off to sleep.

It is peaceful now, as peaceful as peaceful gets.

Suddenly, I hear a terrible cry in the night, the kind of sound that sends shivers up and down a camping parent's spine.

"I have to go to the bathroom!"

* * *

THE CAMP BATHROOM: The camp bathroom is a grungy plywood shack, probably 80 years old, in a sad state of repair. That's not to say it isn't very nice.

The kids don't spend a lot of time in the camp bathroom, however, because the toilet sits over a hole 20 feet in the ground and they believe there are alligators down there.

And who is to know really if there are or aren't alligators in camp toilets because no one has ever really checked.

Let's just say Dad doesn't spend a lot of time in the camp bathroom either.

* * *

GOING TO SLEEP AGAIN: Back in the tent, the kids pile on one another like sled dogs and finally fall asleep.

I, on the other hand, get into this pre-sleep think sequence where I worry that it is too cold and that the kids are all going to freeze and how am I going to explain to their mother when we get home that her children have lost all their fingers and toes to frostbite and that they will never again be able to squeeze the toothpaste or kick a soccer ball, and while I am thinking about all this I finally fall to sleep. Real sleep. Wilderness sleep.

This turns out to be the worst thing I could do to my fellow campers.

Remember your father's snoring, that subhuman sound that rattled the nails loose in the house? Well, that's me. Or so I've been told.

The ensuing conversation in our little tent, I hear later, goes something like this.

Son: "Can't you make him stop snoring?"

Oldest daughter: "He worked so hard today on this camping trip."

Son: "So?"

Oldest daughter: "So I hate to wake him."

Youngest daughter: "I'll bet if you put this sock in his mouth, that would make him stop snoring."

But for some reason, a rare sort of kindness envelopes them and they decide not to wake me. This kindness lasts about 45 seconds.

Son: "Dad! Dad!!"

Me: "Huh? What? Huh?"

Oldest daughter: "You were snoring, Dad."

Me: "I'll roll over. It usually stops when I roll over."

Son: "Thanks, Dad."

Me: " 'Night, everyone."

Everyone: " 'Night, Dad."

Youngest daughter: "Dad?"

Me: "Yes, honey?"

Youngest daughter: "I have to go to the bathroom."

August 18, 1996

◆ ◆ ◆

Nothing Wrong With His Appetite

WE'RE at the Great American Grocery store, checking out this new gust of inflation that's threatening to sweep the nation – eyeing the boneless rib-eyes and the Norwegian salmon, two of my favorite economic indicators.

"How about some salmon?" I ask my wife.

"Too expensive," she says, sounding like Greenspan.

I push the grocery cart onward, leaning low on the handle the way husbands do, slow-dancing the cart past racks of pastries and bags of Halloween candy.

It's harvest time, a bad time for inflation to make a comeback, with taffy apples everywhere and big bags of walnuts. Gourds. Raspberries. Stove-top stuffing. Fixings for a Sunday feast.

"How about some stuffing?" I ask my wife.

"No," she says, not looking up from the list.

I am here to help, though I am not much help. At one time, when the children were very young, I did all the grocery shopping. Now, the most I usually do is run for milk.

But hobbled by a broken foot, my wife needed someone to push the cart. Unfortunately, the boy and I volunteered.

"What's that?" she asks.

"Cream soda," I say.

"Cream soda's good," the boy explains.

"Did you have lunch?" my wife asks, worried that I'm trying to buy everything I see.

"Dad ate lunch twice," the boy tells her.

"Oh, my God," she says.

"Thanks," I tell him.

They say you shouldn't shop when you're hungry, but I am always hungry. Not constantly ravenous or anything. It's just that I could always eat a little something. At all times. Except for the 25 minutes after Thanksgiving dinner, I am always hungry.

So to turn the boy and me loose in a store like this is not the wisest move. You want inflation? We'll give you inflation. Just hand us a shopping cart.

"What's that?" I ask the boy as he sneaks something into the cart.

"Pistachios," he says.

"Smart choice," I say.

"Thanks," he says.

My wife and I turn down an aisle. The boy follows close behind. When his mother's back is turned, he slips in boxes of blueberry Snak-Stix and Hungry Man dinners. When his back is turned, I put them back. Not all of them. Just the stuff I don't like.

"What are you two doing?" my wife asks.

"Overstimulating the economy," I say.

"What?" the boy asks.

"Just push the cart," I tell him.

The boy proves to be an eager shopper. He stops to squeeze the plastic pumpkins. He stops to sample the free breakfast sausage. For five minutes, he browses the chocolate fudge.

"Fudge?" the boy asks.

"Why not?" I say, grabbing a jar.

Eventually, my wife is able to herd us toward the vegetable section, where we are less of a threat to the family budget, sheep-dogging us with her crutches, elbowing us with her elbows.

She's a small woman, but quick and surprisingly strong, like Walter Payton in his prime, mixing speed and power and incredible grace in a way the world seldom sees. Even on a pair of creaky wooden crutches, she is a formidable player.

"Ouch," the boy says.

"What's wrong?" I ask.

"She stepped on my foot," the boy says.

"Over there," she orders, throwing me a shoulder.

"Where?" I say.

"To the eggplant," she says.

For two minutes, I squeeze the eggplant, not really knowing what to feel for but concentrating just the same, my fingertips raw and sensitive from too much remote control. Red Sox. Braves. Bears. They've all taken their toll.

"This one feels pretty good," I tell my wife.

"Try another one," she says, not knowing the pain I'm in.

"Over here, Dad!" the boy yells, waving from the deli counter.

As most men know, there are certain magnetic fields at work inside a grocery store. Beer pulls you one way. Beef pulls you another.

But the deli counter is strongest of all. Chicken, tamales, three kinds of potato salad – all ready to go, all stuff we could eat on the way home.

"We don't need any of this," my wife warns us right away.

"We need it all, Mom," says the boy.

The boy stares at the baked beans and the smoked sausage, his nose nearly touching the steamy glass.

"Have the kids been eating the bologna?" my wife asks.

"I've been eating the bologna," I tell her.

The deli clerk looks at her. The deli clerk looks at me.

"It's very good bologna," I assure the deli clerk.

"Thank you," the deli clerk says proudly.

And finally we make it to the register, where two cashiers are discussing the best place to shoot a misbehaving boyfriend, in the leg or in the hip, finally deciding on the hip for reasons that are unclear to us.

The boy and I stand there uncomfortably, shifting from one leg to the other as we start to unload the cart, careful not to offend anybody.

"Yeah, the hip," one woman says, and they both laugh.

And little by little, the stuff rolls past my wife, the stuff she didn't know we had. Cans of Easy Cheese. Boxes of crackers.

It is harvest food, the kind of stuff men gravitate toward in October. Food for fall Sundays and festive Monday nights. Packers-Bears. Vikings-49ers. For them, we buy this food.

"Easy Cheese?" my wife asks as a can of processed cheese whizzes by.

"It's easy. It's cheese," I say. "Easy Cheese."

"Perfect," says the boy.

October 20, 1999

◆ ◆ ◆

At the Laker Game

I have a beer in hand. A Staples Center beer, 30 cents a sip. Nonetheless, I am content. At 30 cents a sip, you'd better savor every stinkin' bubble. I settle in my overpriced seat and lick mustard from my thumb.

"I am," I tell the boy, "officially happy."

"Look how big Tim Duncan is," the boy says.

"Maybe later," I say.

We get to Staples early because, well, we don't get here very often, the way Jack and Dustin do. The way Dyan Cannon does, an actress/milkshake straw who evidently eats only birdseed and nuts, and not too much of that.

No, we're relative newcomers here to Staples, and it shows. The boy and I are like two farmers visiting the White House for the first time, necks craning, heads always tilted up as we mutter, "Jeesh, it's big." Or "Hey, how 'bout them ceilings?" Stuff like that.

"This," the boy says holding up his sandwich, "is the best sandwich I've ever eaten."

"This," I say, holding up the beer, "is the best beer I've ever had."

Let the game begin.

Oh, right, there's a game here. Staples is, after all, just a giant gymnasium, though it has no discernible musk the way a good gym should – sweat, Pepsi and shellac.

Maybe it's all these sweet-scented Laker Girls, doing moves that would've made Elvis blush.

Or maybe it's all these schmoozers and shakers. Penny Marshall over here. Jeffrey Katzenberg over there. What does a celebrity smell like? I don't know, but it's got to be better than a gym.

In fact, near as we can tell, the boy and I are the only two non-celebrities at Staples on this fine Sunday.

Which works out OK for us, being the last two unfamous people in L.A., though in this lovely and odd little town, that's bound to attract attention on its own.

"What did you do," some interviewer is bound to ask, "to attract so little attention?"

"Nothing," I'll answer.

"That's for sure," the boy will say.

"How 'bout them ceilings?" I'll marvel, and the poor interviewer will move on.

We came here in a hurry, left the house two hours before game time with plans to stop at Philippe's for lunch then move on to Staples for dessert.

But that didn't work out so well, since it was Cinco de Mayo and Chinatown was clogged. We inched toward Philippe's, then stopped cold. Only in L.A. does Chinatown clog up on Cinco de Mayo, near a restaurant named Philippe's.

"Let's get out of here," I said, and spun the wheel, which put us on Broadway, then 8th Street, then Hope. Just when traffic looks bleakest, there's always Hope, itself clogged for some movie shoot.

"We'll never get there," said the boy.

"We're three blocks away," I said.

It's the boy's first Laker game – a playoff game, no less – and he's anxious to get there early. Wants to watch warmups. Wants to study Shaq's smile.

Talk about smiles. Before the game, the camera zooms in and Shaq's face lights up the place, the face of basketball's reigning court jester, master of the slam funk.

In fact, Shaq is the only sports millionaire who seems able to crack a joke anymore. The only athlete having a good time.

Of course, the joking ends with the opening tipoff. The Lakers, rusty from a long layoff, slog through the first quarter.

"Shaq, you're not a forward," a fan shouts after he dares an 8-footer.

"Hey, Robert, shut up!" says another, after Horry gets a technical.

Fickle, these Laker fans. And shy, too. For the first five minutes, it's as if Laker fans have taken some group Botox injection that has deadened them, removed their wrinkles and soothed their high-priced cares.

"Three-peat!" screams the boy, and I swear there was an echo.

For the Lakers' woes continue. They dribble the ball off their shoes and seem to gang up on one side of the basket, look across court to find no one they know, then desperately ricochet a shot off the rim, where it clangs like a horse-shoe. It is basketball so awkward and ugly that actual boos finally ring out across Staples.

At courtside, Nicholson – possibly the Lakers' most ardent fan – grabs the sides of his silvered head and twirls, spins like that McMurphy character he played in "Cuckoo's Nest." Spins like a madman.

"Look at Nicholson," I tell the boy.

"Where?"

And I point out Nicholson in his regular seat along the Spurs' bench, a home-court advantage if there ever was one.

Imagine coming in from Cleveland or Memphis and looking over to see Nicholson three seats away, hair jutting out from the sides of his head like crab grass? Imagine what that does to your game?

In the second period, Heather Locklear arrives, and the Lakers respond with new ferocity, though it might've been a mere coincidence.

At one point, Kobe Bryant, the original Spider-Man, grabs Duncan's head like a bus strap, then soars over the Spurs' star for a slam dunk.

The third quarter is when most of the bloodshed occurs. Shaq gashes his finger, leaves the game to visit his tailor, then returns, darned like a sock.

In the fourth, Kobe leaves. Then Kobe returns. It's like one of Shakespeare's farces, where every 30 seconds someone leaves and two new guys show up.

"You stink, Parker!" a fan yells at the Spurs' Paris-born guard. "You stink, you French poodle!"

I am standing. The boy is standing. Jack is standing. Best of all, the Lakers are still standing, on bruised knees, the defending champs.

"Three-peat!" yells the now lively crowd, on its feet and screaming for yet another NBA title.

"Three-peat!" yells the boy, officially happy at his first Laker game, here at Staples Center, gymnasium to the stars.

May 8, 2002

CHAPTER FOUR

THE LITTLE GIRL

◆ ◆ ◆

A Kindergartner in Training

IT'S three days until the start of kindergarten, and I'm preparing the little red-haired girl for her entry into the outside world.

"You know, everybody thinks the other guy married into more money than they did," I say. "And you know what? I think it's usually true."

But the little red-haired girl says nothing. No nod. No smile. Nothing. She doesn't even offer me a slice of the orange she's eating, which is what I'd really like.

I guess that's L.A. for you. So much sunshine, so little warmth. Even from the ones you love.

A minute later, a tiny hand reaches across the picnic blanket and hands me a slice of the orange.

"Thanks, baby," I tell the little red-haired girl.

Can I leave a nice moment like this alone? Fat chance.

"Now when you get to kindergarten, don't put your mouth on the drinking fountain," I tell her, heaping on more advice. "That's like kissing people you don't even know."

"Sure, Dad," she says with a giggle. The little red-haired girl ends every sentence with a giggle. It's how you know she's done talking.

Is she ready for kindergarten? Who knows? She has a backpack and a lunch kit. She has her first-day outfit all picked out. She can recite the alphabet and the Dodgers' starting lineup. She can tie her shoes.

But is she ready for kindergarten?

By almost any measure, she's a pretty typical 5-year-old. Tall as a baseball bat, she's got hair the color of Hawaiian Punch and a sprinkling of freckles across her nose. A lot of people seem to think she's pretty adorable. Me, I haven't really noticed.

Like a lot of 5-year-olds, she's skinny as a tulip. Just last week, she tried on her new soccer uniform, and before she could get to the mirror, the soccer shorts slipped down to her ankles.

Her older sister, who knows a little something about fashion, explained the problem this way:

"She's got no butt."

"No butt?" the little red-haired girl asked.

"That's right," the older sister said. "How can she keep her soccer shorts up when she doesn't even have a butt?"

"She's butt-impaired!" screamed her 10-year-old brother, who knows a little something about butt jokes.

This led to the usual round of raucous laughter that occurs whenever the word "butt" is mentioned in our house.

"Believe me, she'll grow into her butt," I told them.

"When?"

"When she's good and ready," I said.

"She's butt-impaired!" screamed her brother again, just in case someone on a distant planet didn't hear him the first time.

The little red-haired girl handled the situation as well as possible.

She giggled.

"Is she ready for kindergarten?" I asked her preschool teacher this question last spring.

"Kindergarten?" the teacher answered. "She's ready for college."

Yeah, but I didn't mean that stuff. I didn't mean the counting and the little bit of reading. I meant the other stuff. The stuff that happens outside the classroom. The bully stuff. The taunting on the playground. The looting of lunch kits. That stuff.

"First-graders like to pick on kindergartners," the little red-haired girl says, as if reading my mind. "But I don't care."

"Why not?"

"Because my brother is in the fifth grade," she says. "He could crush a first-grader."

She chomps down on the last piece of orange. The juice squirts me in the side of the head.

"Sorry," she says, then giggles.

Three more days. In three more days, she's not really ours anymore. She belongs to the village. In three days, she'll be subjected to all the bad words and nasty habits known by all the other little villagers.

Not that she'll soak them up necessarily. Just because her older brother and sister did doesn't mean she will. Maybe she will be above that. Maybe pigs will fly.

"You ready for kindergarten?" I ask.

She shrugs and rests her head on my shoulder. The sunlight is fading and so is she. She stretches her legs out over the picnic blanket and slips her thumb into her mouth. Jeesh, she still sucks her thumb. How can she be ready for kindergarten?

I watch her face. She seems smaller than ever. She seems smaller by the moment.

We notice a tiny brown ant crawling up her shoe. The ant crosses her sock and heads for a teardrop of orange juice on her knee.

"Look at that stupid ant," she says.

"How do you know it's stupid?" I ask. "Maybe it's a smart ant."

She reaches down and smacks the ant, crushing it with her palm.

"Stupid ant," she says with a giggle.

She's ready for kindergarten.

October 6, 1996

♦ ♦ ♦

The Soccer Ref's Fan

So I'm standing in the middle of a soccer field, watching a 6-year-old goal-keeper hold the ball over his head with both hands.

The 6-year-old goalkeeper has no intention of throwing the ball. He has no intention of doing anything. Because as he holds the ball, about 40 people are yelling at him. And he's never had 40 people yelling at him before.

"Throw it over here!" someone yells.

"Throw it over there!" someone else yells.

For more than a minute, the goalie holds the ball over his head. The longer he holds it, the more people yell. And the more people yell, the less he's inclined to throw it.

"Just throw the ball!" yells his coach, spinning around and flapping his arms like a duck, the way coaches do when things aren't going well.

As the referee, I am standing right in front of the little boy with the ball. I can see in his eyes that he has no intention of throwing this ball. He is frozen. There is nothing wrong, really. He's just frozen.

It happens to 6-year-old soccer players all the time. Sometimes, they just freeze. There is so much going on, so much stuff to remember about footwork and yard lines and where to throw the ball, that 6-year-old soccer players just freeze.

It can really stir up the fans.

"What's wrong?" asks a grandmother along the sideline.

"He's frozen," a parent says.

"Hey, kid, throw the ball!" the grandmother yells.

I can't blame the kid for not throwing the ball. All this screaming could confuse anybody. So after two or three minutes, I blow the whistle.

"Let me see that ball," I say.

The goalkeeper hands me the ball. I look at it, as if examining it for defects, then toss it over my shoulder and back into the middle of the playing field.

"Play on!" I yell.

The two teams chase the ball, and the game begins again.

"Nice throw," the goalie says.

"Thanks," I say.

Today's game features two of the finest teams in soccer. On one side, we have the Flying Monkeys of the Apocalypse. On the other, the Purple Slime. Both sides play a clean, smart game. Both sides know what they're doing. Only occasionally do players actually leave the ground like human missiles and fling themselves at the other team with the intent of entirely destroying them. In those cases, I blow my whistle.

"What's that, ref?" the coach yells.

"That's a penalty," I say.

"What for?"

"For being a human missile," I say.

"Oh," the coach says.

As you might guess from their name, the Flying Monkeys of the Apocalypse are the more aggressive of the two teams. From the opening whistle, the Flying Monkeys begin to kick.

They march down the field like redcoats, shoulder to shoulder, kicking anything that gets in their way. Sometimes, they kick the ball. Other times, they kick each other. Sometimes, they just stand in one place and kick at the air, waiting for something better to come along.

They are a close team. If a player goes down, they graciously bend down and pick him up by his ears, the way Lyndon Johnson used to pick up hunting dogs.

"Thanks," the player says.

"For what?"

"For picking me up by my ears," the player says.

As I ref, the little red-haired girl sits along the sideline and watches me work. When her game is over, her dad/coach has to referee the next game, and usually she stays to watch.

She likes the way her dad refs soccer games, running up and down the field in his relaxed-fit jeans, tugging at the waistband every few steps to keep them from falling. He runs like a fat guy fleeing a fire, his arms flailing, his ref's whistle bouncing up and down on his chest.

Up and back he goes. Sometimes the soccer ball ricochets off his legs, but he just keeps running. Up and back, up and back.

She thinks it's great, the way he refs. Funny and great. Sometimes, she actually cheers for him.

"Good call, ref!" she yells. Or, "Nice jeans, Dad!"

Nobody much cheers for refs, which she doesn't really understand, because watching her daddy ref is one of the greatest spectacles in sports.

He's a good ref, she says. He constantly makes her laugh, the way he stumbles over the water bottles along the sideline, holding up his pants and dodging Flying Monkeys all at the same time. He makes it look easy, the way good refs do.

"That's my dad out there," she proudly tells her friends.

"What's wrong with his pants?" one of them asks.

"I don't know," says the little red-haired girl. "But he sure can ref."

December 1, 1997

◆ ◆ ◆
Paradise in Her Eyes

AND into Miami we go, full of unreasonable expectations of what a vacation should be, hoping for Acapulco but getting South Florida instead. So Flo. Viagra Falls. First stop for fugitive investors and retired grandmothers.

"I like it here," says the little girl.

"Me too," I say.

What's not to like? Miami has recovered nicely from all that Cuba boy business. Mayor Gloria Estefan has given up politics for now and returned to show business. It's a good time to be visiting South Florida. Everywhere you look, there are signs of hope. Everywhere you look, there's a grandma.

"There's one," says the little girl, pointing out the car window.

"Actually, that's a grandpa," her older sister tells her.

She counts grandmas the way some kids count Volkswagen Beetles. She's got two grandmas down here but could probably have as many as she wanted. A hundred grandmas, passing her from lap to lap at condo association meetings, running their fingers through her hair.

Yep, Miami is paradise in her eyes. Full of grandparents and parrot jungles. Alligator farms. Nice rental cars.

"When are we going shark hunting?" asks the boy.

"Maybe tomorrow," I say.

"I want to go para-sailing," says my lovely and patient older daughter.

South Florida is a tough place to pin down. There are miles of condos, stacked like sugar cubes along the beaches, the buzz of air-conditioning units filling the heavy air.

There is hyper-hip Miami Beach, a world-class beach city, sleepy by day but alive all night.

And there is the usual array of exotic Florida attractions, alligator farms, parrot jungles, jai-alai frontons, beautiful racetracks and hundreds of pawnshops, handy as 7-Elevens.

It is a fascinating and maddening place, even if you've lived here before and know how to get around, as we do. Even if your reflexes are still fairly quick.

"Watch out, Dad," says my older daughter as another driver crosses three lanes to exit.

South Florida has always tested your traffic skills, but now Viagra boils in the bloodstream of about half the drivers. Maybe it's my imagination, but it appears to have created an aggressive, slashing style of driving. Drivers under the influence of Viagra. DUVs.

"Look at that," I tell my wife as a red Oldsmobile plows into a shopping cart.

"Oh, God," she says.

"I'll bet that old guy's full of Viagra," I say.

"Oh, he's probably just blind," she explains.

"Probably both," my older daughter says.

"What's Viagra?" asks the little girl.

"Love medicine," explains the boy, who knows a thing or two about love.

Lucky for us, there is always something to do here in South Florida. We drive around visiting in-laws. We play golf. We head to the beach, where the surf is 87 degrees, warm as a cup of tea.

Anything you'd catch in these Gulfstream waters would likely be pre-cooked. Lobster. Scallops. Toss in some potatoes and you'd have a full meal.

Especially in August. In August, Miami cooks in its own juices. For hours, we lie around the hotel pool and the beach, sweating profusely and reapplying sunscreen. Thick as clown makeup, this sunscreen, full of the waxes that make it waterproof.

"More," my wife urges as I paint myself white.

"More?"

"More," she says.

Doesn't matter. This is Florida sun. It not only penetrates the sunscreen, it passes through my body like X-rays, glancing off my gallbladder and then igniting several jai-alai ticket stubs under my lounge chair.

In 15 minutes, my spleen is sunburned. After 20 minutes, I'm starting to feel it in my liver.

"I think my pancreas is burning," I tell my wife.

"You should turn over," she says.

One afternoon, I escape the heat and humidity by watching soap operas with my stepmother-in-law.

"I'm going to the boardroom now," one of the soap opera characters says.

"The boardroom," my stepmother-in-law explains. "That's where all the crooks are."

"Just like in real life," I say.

"These shows are very realistic," she says.

Watching soap operas with my stepmother-in-law is like watching Monday Night Football with Joe Montana. She knows all the players. She knows all the inside stuff.

"He's a rich kid and a bad guy," she explains when they cut to a handsome young man in a hospital bed. "His dad's a bad guy too."

"Just like real life," I say.

The handsome young man in the hospital bed is hearing some bad news. I can't tell what. Maybe he's being sent to South Florida. Or L.A. He's taking it hard, whatever it is.

The guy grimaces. He's got one of those abnormally large Adam's apples that bobs up and down when he's worked up. Like a goiter, this thing. If I watch too closely, I get dizzy. Fortunately, my son stops by just as I'm about to fall out of my father-in-law's favorite chair.

"Dad, when are we going to hunt sharks?" the boy asks again.

"My spear gun's in the shop," I tell him.

"Then why'd we come down here?" he asks.

"To eat crab," I say. "And visit your grandparents."

"Mom says the crab places are closed for summer," he says.

"Now you tell me," I say.

On TV, the guy with the Adam's apple swallows hard.

August 16, 2000

◆ ◆ ◆

The Playoffs

I enter the dugout like Mr. Magoo, stumbling over bats and bumping into everyone. By George, there's a game here somewhere. A playoff game. You can imagine the pressure.

"Over here, girls," I tell the team. "Everybody over here."

And the little girls put down their snacks and huddle around me and the other two coaches, 12 talented young players eager to get on with things.

"Everybody feeling good today?" I ask.

Several of them nod.

"Then let's put our hands in," I say.

We all join hands for a team yell. This is where it gets serious. This is where you know it's really the playoffs.

"Let's win this game," I say softly, "for the moms."

"Our moms?" someone asks.

"All the moms," I say seriously.

The players all look at me. I can tell I struck a chord with this moms thing. Tears well. Several lower lips quiver, especially Coach Bill's.

"Let's win it for the moms!" says Coach Lorraine, a mom herself.

It is, perhaps, the most shameless motivational ploy since the Gipper speech. Frankly, I don't care. Did I mention it's the playoffs?

* * *

SECOND INNING:

"Don't hit any of those bouncy pitches," I tell the little girl as she gets ready to hit.

"OK, Dad," she says.

Twice this season, the little girl has singled on pitches that bounced 3 feet in front of the plate, digging the ball out of the dirt as if swinging a sand wedge.

"This time, wait for a good pitch," I tell her, guiding her gently by the shoulders toward the plate.

I send her from the dugout as if releasing a prize fish back into a stream. Carefully. Slowly. She wriggles from my hands and into the batter's box.

"Strike One," the umpire says, and the little girl looks over at me standing in the dugout door, giving me the look that says, "That wasn't a strike, was it? How could that be a strike? I wasn't even ready. That was no strike."

"Strike Two!" the umpire says, before she has time to get set again.

"Anything close now," I tell the little girl, warning her to swing at anything resembling a strike.

"Anything close," I say again.

The next pitch comes in a little low. About midway to the plate, it rolls a couple of times, then hits a rock and takes a hop, arriving right at the little girl's ankles. Right where she likes them.

"Nice hit," I mumble as she dances on first base.

* * *

THIRD INNING:

"This other team has some real players," I tell Coach Bill.

"Which team?" he asks.

"The team we're playing," I say.

"You don't say."

We have these conversations, Coach Bill and I. The subject of the conversation is never clear right away, if ever.

Mostly, they sound like some old Rowan & Martin bit, where stuff is happening all around us, the Sock-It-to-Me Girl is out there dancing and Arte Johnson is falling off his tricycle. Those are the kinds of conversations we have.

"Hey, Caitlin, move to the right a little more!" Bill yells to Caitlin at second base.

"She takes direction well," I tell Bill.

"Who?" he asks.

"Caitlin," I tell him.

"What about her?"

Meanwhile, there are unconfirmed reports that one of the other team's coaches is gazing at our first base coach's legs. That'd be Coach Lorraine. Plays a lot of tennis. Married to a successful fertility specialist. So you can just imagine.

Nevertheless, several of our mothers are pretty upset by all this leering, which they find rude and out of place, especially since it's directed at someone besides themselves.

"That one coach," one of the wives hisses through the chain-link dugout, "keeps looking at Lorraine's legs."

"She's got nice legs," Coach Bill says, as if noticing for the first time.

"The best in baseball," I say.

"I thought I had the best legs in baseball," Coach Bill says.

"That was last year," I tell him. "Things change."

* * *

FOURTH INNING:

Last inning and we need five runs.

"Strike One!" yells the umpire.

The other team is striking out many of our players. One by one, they go down swinging.

"Anybody here Catholic?" one of our players asks. "Anybody?"

I don't know if she's looking for someone to pray with, or just curious about our various religious affiliations.

"Strike Two!" yells the umpire.

"So I'm the only Catholic?" asks Kathleen, who's as tiny as a hymnal.

"My dad was Catholic," I tell her.

"OK," she says, seemingly relieved.

Despite the tension, our fans in the stands appear to be unnaturally happy, particularly for parents.

There are fits of raucous laughter coming from our stands. A yelp. A scream. Then more laughter.

"What's going on over there?" someone asks.

"I think they're drinking happy juice," Coach Bill says.

"They're not supposed to be drinking happy juice," I say.

"I'll go check it out," says Coach Lorraine, a stickler for rules.

Occasionally at games like these, you hear reports of happy juice being served. I've never seen it, but I don't doubt it happens. I'm 43. Nothing surprises me anymore.

"Did you warn them?" I ask Coach Lorraine when she returns.

"Yes," she says.

"And what'd they say?"

"They said I have really nice legs."

June 7, 2000

Mom's Personal Assistant

So it's early, early Tuesday and I'm ironing my wife's shirt despite this pain in my neck, which probably seems superhuman except that this is what today's husbands do – iron shirts in an emergency, even when we're hurt. Keeps us at the forefront of daily life while preventing the complete motherization of America. At home, at work, on the ball field, mothers are taking over and creating a more perfect world, despite our innate male disdain for perfection. Goodbye, Bobby Knight. So long, Hugh Hefner parties. Hello, perfection.

"Mom wants to know if her shirt is done," some kid asks as I iron.

"In a minute," I say.

On the right side of my neck, there is a sharp pain. Farther up, there is a screw loose. I'm not sure where. When I shake my head, I hear the screw rattle. I think it's near my oil pan.

"What are you doing?" the boy asks as he grabs something off the dryer.

"I'm ironing," I say.

"You are?" he asks.

"You got a problem with that?" I ask.

The boy tries to resist a smile, but you know how that goes. He smiles. He doesn't smile. He smiles. He doesn't smile.

The boy seems to know that you don't make fun of a guy who's ironing. Because he's already a little edgy.

"Well, you're doing a good job, Dad," he finally says, then laughs to his room.

"Later, pal," I mutter under my breath. "Later."

I iron this shirt for five minutes before realizing that the iron is not on. I thought that when you plugged irons in, they went on. Who would plug in an iron if you didn't want it on? In a sense, it's like a TV.

So I turn the iron on. Then I look at the shirt label. The shirt is made of cotton and linen. The cotton makes up 45% of the fibers. Linen, the rest. Made in Sri Lanka, this shirt. It's a little tricky around the collar, as Sri Lankan shirts often are.

"What are you doing, Dad?" my lovely and patient older daughter asks.

"Reevaluating my life," I tell her.

"That should be set to cotton blend," she tells me, looking at the iron.

"Thanks."

"Can you iron my green shirt?" she asks.

"Don't push your luck," I say.

Good as he was, I don't remember my father doing much ironing. Or picking up a dirty dish. Or diapering a baby. It was a different time. Dads left in the morning; moms stayed home. Now both do both. In a sense, we're working twice as hard.

Of course, it doesn't help to have those "Sex and the City" girls running all over the place, giving people ideas.

"Dad?" the little girl says.

"Huh?"

"Mom needs her shirt," she says.

It bothers me a little that the mother didn't come ask for the shirt herself. Instead, she sends one of these young personal assistants that mothers have these days, cheeky kids with a little too much confidence. The kind of kid who got Bob Knight in trouble.

"Tell her it's on the way," I tell the little girl.

"When?" the little girl asks.

"When it's ready," I say.

You know, for a while, life as a guy is good. You start out as Holden Caulfield, then segue for about 10 seconds into Gatsby, young and all-seeing and desperate for love. Which can only lead to trouble. Major trouble.

Sure enough, before long you're married and middle-aged. Suddenly, you're not desperate for love anymore, just your youth and a decent night's rest.

So you make the best of things, as guys always do. You grab an ironing board and a shirt and think about the spread on the UCLA game and how you have to get the oil changed Saturday before kickoff.

You make a mental list of all the things you have to do. Point spreads and oil changes. That's about it. Since you're a guy, your mental list of things to do is very fluid. Only you control it. People are always trying to add things to your mental list, yet you reject them. Not everything. Just the superfluous stuff.

"Got it," you say, then forget it on purpose.

Still, stuff slips through. It's the ugly underbelly of our raging economy, these things husbands do so their wives can be super productive. The government doesn't index it. Basically, it's immeasurable what we do. The extra effort. The ironing.

"How's this look?" I ask the little personal assistant, holding up the ironed shirt.

"Not so good," she says.

"Did I mention my neck hurts?" I say.

"Daddy, are you OK?"

"Never better," I say.

But I explain to her that when she gets to be middle-aged, she'll have these nagging little morning aches and pains that used to disappear but don't. She'll probably have to wear a knee brace when she works out. At the dentist, she'll hear about gum disease.

"And it's never too soon to start thinking about life insurance," I tell her.

"I want life insurance," she says.

"That's the spirit," I tell her.

The more I tell the little girl about middle age, the more excited she becomes. By the time I get to company 401(k) plans, she's ready to move into middle age today. Preferably, a middle-management position.

"How long till I'm middle-aged?" she asks, envy in her voice.

"About 35 years," I tell her.

"That's a long time," she says.

"Not really," I say, then hand her the shirt.

The little girl races to her mother with the shirt. It's 6:55 in the morning. Everybody's late.

I unplug the iron, then glance at the dirty breakfast dishes. In a minute, the little girl comes running back waving the shirt.

"Starch," she says.

"Never heard of it," I say.

"Starch," she says, pointing to the Niagara.

As she watches, I spray starch on the collar, then down the front of the shirt. Then on my hand and leg. It's a good feeling. Kind of tingly.

"Oops," I say, looking at my starched leg.

"You OK, Dad?" she asks.

"Did I mention my neck hurts?" I say.

September 20, 2000

◆ ◆ ◆

The Little Girl's First Wedding

HERE, on the very edge of America's left coast, someone is about to get married – 200 steps from the slurping Pacific, on a bluff overlooking the ocean. It's an outdoor wedding. The bride is wearing white. The ocean, Dodger blue.

"Nice place for a wedding," I say, without too much irony in my voice.

"This is beautiful," says my wife.

We are so close to the edge of the continent that one crash of a phantom wave and the bride and groom would be bodysurfing.

I assume the wedding guests would gather around the bride and groom as they bodysurfed, climb down the bluffs and cheer on the happy couple as they swam off to Santa Barbara for an early honeymoon.

The band would stand out on the bluff and play "The Hokey Pokey" as the guests danced along the water's edge. They'd put their right feet in. They'd put their right feet out. They'd do the hokey pokey and they'd shake it all about. . . .

"Let us pray," says the minister, jolting me out of my daydream.

My prayer? That this cliff holds out. That the marriage does, too. That the ceremony is short and the reception long and just boozy enough to be fun. That they have those portable heaters around the patio reception area. Those are my prayers.

And before you know it, the bride comes down the aisle on her father's arm, and all the little girls in the audience turn to look. For some of them, it is their first wedding. Magic is in the air. And a touch of sea mist. A twist of lime.

It's spring, a good time for a wedding. Back home, the boy's pet rabbit is in heat, hurling herself at the top of the cage and moaning like a teenager. Must be bunny lust. Must be spring.

"What's wrong with the bunny?" the little girl constantly asks her mother.

"She's crazy," the boy says.

"She's in love," her mother says.

"Same thing," I say.

It's spring, and the sparrows are nesting in the eaves in the back of the house. It's spring, and my friend Irv is running off to Vegas to get married. Just like that, without telling anyone.

There is a rampant, terrifying romance in the air, surf-like and pounding in our ears.

On TV, men and women are chaining themselves together in the name of love, which is weird, even as courtships go.

With all that in mind, we come here to the ocean's edge. To a wedding. The ultimate survival show.

"You may be seated," the minister says, and I sit quickly, like a drunk on a stagecoach.

I have been married only once, a huge success in my eyes, but a tossup in the eyes of anyone who knew my wife beforehand.

But I have attended a hundred such ceremonies. In my mind, almost all weddings fit into one of three major categories.

1. The frat boy wedding: Where all the groomsmen look like ESPN anchor boys and the bridesmaids look like Hooters girls. For a month before the ceremony, everyone diets, including the groom. Nobody talks about what happened at the bachelor party. Nobody. Because nobody can really remember. Life expectancy of such a marriage: 15 months.

2. The we've-got-money wedding: An elegant and formal occasion, where the main purpose is to display how much money the bride's parents have. There are trumpet flourishes. Peacocks. Eight maids a-milking. Seven lords a-leaping. A mother-in-law in a pear tree, roaring drunk. Life expectancy of such a marriage: 20 years (or as long as the dowry lasts).

3. The simple, just-friends wedding: Thrown together like a barbecue. Chips. Dip. Brewskies in the cooler. On TV, a ballgame. No band, but around 11, someone throws an old Aerosmith album on the stereo. Life expectancy of

such a marriage: 30 years to life.

Fortunately, tonight's wedding falls into none of these categories, which means I have to pay attention. I cannot sleep. If I sleep, I might roll into the ocean, ruining my best and only suit.

"There goes Dad," the little girl would say as I rolled out of my chair and off the cliff.

"And his hundred-dollar suit," her mother would say, then turn back to the ceremony.

The evening is a little cool but otherwise perfect. The minister is witty. Casual. It's a California wedding. The participants look like they work outside, healthy and tanned.

Midway through the ceremony, my wife glances over to make sure I am still awake. While the minister speaks of love, commitment and honor, she looks at me.

I know exactly what she's thinking. "When did he turn into Bob Newhart?" is what she's thinking. "When did he grow ear hair like a mongoose?"

What am I thinking? "At the reception, I hope they have those little meatball appetizers," is what I'm thinking. "Hope I don't have to dance too much."

Up at the altar, meanwhile, this fine, tasteful wedding ceremony is winding down. The groomsmen are relaxed now, thinking about a nice glass of Merlot and tomorrow's golf match.

The bridesmaids are thinking about the groomsmen.

The little girl, two chairs down, is thinking she's never seen anyone so beautiful as her second-grade teacher – all in white up there at the altar, with the ocean deep and blue behind her.

Good luck, Miss Hamrick, the little girl is thinking. Good luck, forever.

April 25, 2001

◆ ◆ ◆

How to Read the Sports Pages

BUTLER had three hits, the little red-haired girl tells me. "In two at-bats."

"That's impossible," I say.

"Says right here," she insists, pointing to the box score.

It's Sunday morning, and I'm teaching the little red-haired girl how to read the Sports section.

Like a lot of beginners, she tends to start with the first page, then work her way inside. But I am teaching her the proper way to read the Sports, turning to the box scores first, then the standings, then working her way back to the cover page, saving Jim Murray for last, kind of like dessert.

"When I was your age, Jim Murray was God," I tell her. "And you know what? He's still God. Forget Grantland Rice and Red Smith. Jim Murray is the greatest American sportswriter."

"Sure, Dad," she says, rolling her eyes and turning to the American League standings.

Talking to a dad about baseball is like talking about politics with a lunatic, full of passion and loopy observations. It's frightening and funny all at once. And the little red-haired girl eats up every word.

"Dad, tell me again how the Cubs folded in '69 and broke your heart," the 6-year-old says. "Tell me about that."

So I tell her about Santo and Kessinger and how Billy Williams couldn't pull the team together and Ernie Banks was past his prime, which was just really lucky for the Mets, because Ernie Banks in his prime was really something to watch. Willie Mays may have had more talent, but Ernie Banks had more heart. And you should never underestimate heart.

"Ernie who?" she asks.

Poor kid. She learned about baseball by watching her older brother play Little League. Her brother's a pretty good player, of course, but he once spent an entire inning smashing a bumblebee on the dugout bench, then sprinkling it with dirt.

For a while, this turned the little red-haired girl off sports. She assumed all athletes were killers.

"You think your brother's bad?" I tell her. "You should see what the owners do."

"Huh?" she says.

"The owners," I say. "They're ruthless."

"Huh?"

"How about I tell you about the '54 Yankees?" I ask.

"OK."

So we lie back on the couch again, and I tell her about the great New York teams of the '50s, about Berra and Maris and Mantle, some of the finest ballplayers the sport has ever known. In a few minutes, it becomes clear that she's never heard of any of these guys. Not a one.

"You're kidding, right?" I say.

"Nope."

"Where are you from, Mars?"

"Earth," she says.

"Earth? Really? What part exactly?"

She was once a promising young ballplayer herself, this kid, an ingenue of the infield, a princess at the plate. She would slap line drives, then sprint for first base in 100 tiny steps, sometimes stopping to rest, but only if she was really tired. Some compared her to a young Roberto Clemente.

Her finest moment probably came in the first inning of the first game when, chewing four pieces of Bazooka, she blew a bubble roughly the size of a human head.

"It got all over my face," she would later tell sportswriters.

But midway through the season, she went into an awful slump. Suddenly, she couldn't hit the curveball, or the fastball, or any other kind of pitch that the coach softly lobbed to her over and over in endless innings on lumpy school playgrounds.

"Swing the bat!" her big brother would yell to her from behind the backstop. "Just swing the bat!"

He had no sympathy for kids who couldn't hit. A ferocious batter himself, he is known for swinging at almost anything that comes near home plate. Birds. Bees. Even pitches 3 feet over his head.

He once swung at a hummingbird 30 feet away. "It was bothering me," he explained.

So, still stinging from her collapse at the plate, the little red-haired girl decided to take this year off from baseball and concentrate on kindergarten and jumping rope.

And, most of all, learning to read the Sports section.

We are on the last page now, running out of standings, running short of roundups. In spring, a Sports section is in full bloom, with baseball and basketball and Preakness previews. But eventually, even a spring Sports section comes to an end.

So she begins to build a tent, laying the Sports pages, one sheet at a time, across my face and stomach until I am completely covered.

"Is it dark in there?"

"Yeah," I say. "Come on in."

She wiggles in next to me on the couch, past the baseball standings and the weekend TV listings, careful not to crinkle Jim Murray. She may be just a beginner, but she knows you never crinkle Jim Murray.

"Ouch."

"Sorry," she says, apologizing for her bony knees before wiggling in a little closer. "There. Now no one will find us."

I try to breathe through the newsprint. It smells like baseball, this paper, like Dodger Stadium in spring, like Wrigley in July. Or maybe it just smells like newsprint.

"You asleep, Daddy?"

"No, I'm just dreaming."

"Oh," she says. "Want me to tell you about the Cubs?"

"Who?"

"The Cubs," she says. "You know, the Cubbies."

"Sure," I say. "Tell me about those Cubbies."

May 11, 1997

Livin' la Vida Polka

HERE we are headed to Staples Center, L.A.'s grand canyon, a sexy new arena named after an office implement.

"Know where you're going, Pops?" asks the little girl.

"Not really," I say.

"Uh-oh," she says from the back seat.

She's been calling me Pops lately, as if I suddenly turned into Fred MacMurray and smoke a pipe and wear a big cardigan, as if I'm headed through life a little befuddled. Fred MacMurray. I take it for the compliment it is.

"Maybe that's where we turn, Pops," she says, pointing to an exit.

"That's Chinatown," I tell her.

"You sure?" she asks.

"Yeah, I'm sure," I tell her.

And we head on down the Pasadena Freeway to the Harbor, then off quickly to where we expect Staples Center to be. It's our first time here.

"See any signs?" I ask.

"I don't see any signs," my wife says.

We are on our way to see Ricky Martin, of all people, one of pop music's hottest divas – a bonbon-shaking phenom who filled Dodger Stadium this summer and now has his sights set on Staples. Just like us.

"I love that song of his," I tell the little girl.

"Which song?" she asks, as if he has more than one or two.

" 'Livin' la Vida Polka,' " I tell her.

"That's not what it's called," she says.

"It's not?"

"It's 'Livin' la Vida Loca,' " she says.

"I like that one too," I say.

And we park, 20 bucks, then walk across the street to Staples Center.

Now, if you haven't seen Staples, maybe you should. Gleaming, stylish, with lots of windows overlooking downtown.

"I'm feeling a little tingly," I tell my wife as we wander down the shiny hallways.

"That's just the beer," my wife says.

"No, I think it's this place," I tell her.

Though it could be the beer. It's cold and tall, and at $6.75, plenty steep, much like the Staples seating. And the wine is no bargain either.

Amazingly, the bartender has to do the math on a napkin to get the total. $6.75 plus $6.25. Quickly, the tingle subsides.

"That'll impress people from out of town," I say with a sigh.

"Just drink your beer," my wife says.

Up to our seats we go, the three of us, up to meet another family and enjoy the show. Up and up we go, almost a straight climb, up to the top of this grand canyon, holding tight to the railing.

I look down. As one friend noted, it's only a matter of time before some drunk takes a header from these upper-deck seats, straight into the luxury boxes located directly below. Scream. Plop. Scream.

My guess is that it will happen during the fourth quarter of a Laker game, with all the drunk's buddies watching.

"There goes Bill," they'll say, then turn back to the game.

"Luckily, I landed on a stock broker," Bill will explain later from his hospital bed.

Scream. Plop. Scream.

"Keep going, Pops," says the little girl, as I stop to look down at the luxury boxes.

"We're almost there," I say, leading them to Row 11.

And before we know it, Ricky Martin is leaping out on stage, gyrating wildly.

The stage is like some sort of spaceship, with moving sidewalks and a center stage that lifts up and down.

Every once in a while, huge piston-like tubes rise high out of the stage, metaphors for something, I'm not sure. Maybe for car engines.

Then there are these dancers, a dozen at least, gyrating like human washing machines, jumping from level to level, barely stopping to take a breath as Ricky's other hit blasts across the arena.

Shake your bonbon, shake your bonbon, shake your bonbon.

Basically, what these dancers appear to do is stick out their sleek backsides, then swing their long hair around in helicopter fashion as a hundred strobe lights flash. Just watching makes me dizzy.

Shake your bonbon, shake your bonbon, shake your bonbon.

Midway through the show, I take a walk around the upper level, which takes only five or 10 minutes. When I return, I have a hot dog. Come to an arena, have a hot dog – that's my motto.

"How's the hot dog?" the other father asks when I return.

"Pretty hot," I say.

The hot dog cost almost four bucks, though that's not so shocking anymore. A Downtown Dog, they call it. It's served at about a thousand degrees, too hot to hold and put mustard on, let alone eat. Ten minutes later, it is still too hot. Prepared by welders, this dog.

Shake your bonbon, shake your bonbon, shake your bonbon.

Back on stage, the lights dim and Ricky slows it down a little.

The sound is good for so high up, though at times, there is a sort of echo effect. At times, it as though 10,000 children are singing along with him.

I look around, everyone is singing along with him. Ten thousand children. Five thousand young women. A few thousand moms and dads. Almost everyone singing.

"You're not singing," I tell the other father.

"Sorry," he says.

It is no small measure of our lives that this other father and I missed Springsteen here at Staples but somehow wind up watching two hours of Ricky Martin.

And it is no small measure of our lives that this other father and I are glad to be here, appreciating the wild scene and enjoying the music.

You could do worse. Onstage, the dancers return, doing that helicopter thing with their hair.

Up in the stands, the kids are singing.

You could do a lot worse.

November 17, 1999

♦ ♦ ♦

Go, Gigglers!

So I show up at the field looking like soccer's Santa Claus – with a bag full of toys, balls mostly. Me, a guy with freckled legs and Hitler's hairline carrying this giant bag of soccer balls, limping a little. As coaches go, I'm considered fairly attractive.

"OK, girls, over here," I say and limp/lead the team to the warmup area.

Saturday is still wet behind the ears, but here we are, out on this dew-kissed field getting our shoes and socks soaked – all in the name of youth soccer. If there's a better reason, please let me know.

"Did you bring doughnuts?" one of the players asks.

"I brought coffee and cigars," I say.

"I'll take some coffee," one of them says.

"I'll take some coffee, too," says another.

They are always asking for food. Or drinks. Or money. I am not so much their coach as I am their executive producer, responsible for everything in their little lives, responsible for their happiness, their well-being, their sense of self. I do my best, but there is only so much an executive producer can do.

"Where are we going for lunch today, coach?" one of the players says.

"We're not going for lunch," I say.

"Dinner? You're buying dinner?" she asks.

This is how they've gotten now that they're 8 or 9. Like little wise guys. Nothing they say is ever serious. Everything other people say provokes laughter, intended or not.

I can't take any credit for this development. This is just how they behave. Guess we just got lucky.

"Coach is buying dinner!" yells the little red-haired girl, and everyone cheers.

We have been meeting like this since August, the team in the little green and yellow uniforms that remind me of the Green Bay Packers.

"Hey, Packers!" I told my assistant coach, Gary, when he delivered the uniforms.

"I thought they were blue," said coach Gary.

Green. Blue. Doesn't matter. We're the mighty Lightning Bolts. We play to win. Coach Gary and I established that at our first meeting with the girls, way back when.

"I just want to say," I told the team, "that there's a new sheriff in town."

"Where?" asked one of the girls.

"Right here," I said.

"Where?" several others asked, now thoroughly confused.

"Never mind," I said.

As coaches go, I'm considered fairly funny.

So we skipped the pep talk and went right to drills, where we discovered that:

- Four girls had never played soccer before.
- Three girls had played a little soccer but saw the game mostly as a social opportunity.
- Five girls despised soccer but had to come because their mothers made them.

As first practices go, I thought it went very well.

"We stink," said the little girl as we climbed into the car afterward.

"It's too early to tell," I said.

"No, Dad, we really stink," she said.

Indeed, we did stink – at least for the first couple of games. Our players would attack the ball with their eyes closed, taking tiny little geisha steps in the general direction of the action, as if carrying trays of hot tea. If the ball came near, they would turn and carry their trays in the other direction.

"Good try!" the moms all yelled, even when it wasn't.

Then we had a rainout – which was encouraging – followed by two big victories, which was even more encouraging.

Suddenly, in just the past two weeks, the Lightning Bolts are a team on the move. Giddy. Overconfident. As executive producer, I am appropriately worried.

"Quit giggling, girls," I say over and over at our next practice.

"Why?" one of them asks.

"Yeah, why?" says another.

"If you giggle, you're gonna run laps," says coach Gary, prompting convulsing, riotous laughter, during which two of the girls strain ligaments near their rib cages, possibly knocking themselves out for the season.

"What's wrong with them today?" I ask coach Gary as the Lightning Bolts run their laps.

"Winning streak, coach," says coach Gary.

"If we keep winning, we're doomed," I say.

"You said it," he says.

When they return from their laps, the Giggling Bolts fall to the ground and giggle some more. One of them – probably my daughter – entertains them with a story about the time her father tried to order a gin and tonic at the McDonald's drive-thru, confusing the poor clerk/announcer person and embarrassing nearly everybody in the car.

"Can you believe it?" she says, her eyes filling with tears. "A gin and tonic!"

There's some truth to this story, though the details are a little hazy. It was way back in July, I think, and we were on the way home from a wedding. Or a funeral.

" . . . A cheeseburger Happy Meal, four fries and a gin and tonic," I told the announcer/clerk.

"Did he say gin and tonic?" my lovely and patient older daughter asked from the back seat.

"Your father was just kidding," her mother explained.

"Sure I was," I mumbled.

As coaches go, I don't really drink much. Not with the hours I keep, up all night reviewing game film and studying the salary cap. There's just no time.

"Who do we play next week?" one of the players asks as they roll around in the grass discussing gin and tonics.

"The New York Yankees," I say.

"Are they hard?" one of them asks.

"They've got a great owner," I say.

"I wish we did," the little girl says, prompting more waves of laughter. Nausea. Vomiting. And several outbreaks of chicken pox.

"What's so funny?" I whisper to coach Gary.

"Beats me," coach Gary says.

And as the sun goes down, the mighty Lightning Bolts run another lap.

October 11, 2000

Glad to Hear It

WE are always exhausted, my wife and I. Kids. Jobs. Homework. Housework.

The nation's leaders tell us the economy is thriving. But to maintain the lifestyles our parents knew, it now takes two incomes instead of one. And who works 40-hour weeks anymore? The last person to work a mere 40 hours was laid off in 1991.

So in a world of diminishing returns, sometimes it's hard to know what to be thankful for.

But late at night, a room away, I can hear a little boy talking in his sleep. In his dreams, the Dodgers are winning the World Series.

For small comforts like these, I am thankful.

* * *

"Dad, your breasts are crooked."

I was desperate for a Halloween costume. That's how I got the breasts – two balloons tucked underneath an old sweater.

And because accessories are so important, I added a simple strand of pearls. And a blond wig. But it was my full figure everyone fixated on. Big-breasted men tend to have that problem.

"Your left one is pointing straight up," my daughter says. "And your right one . . . oh, Dad."

"You got a problem with that?" I ask, lighting a cigar.

My poor daughter doesn't know whether to laugh or cry.

"I am living someone else's life," she says, rubbing her temples.

"Have any earrings I could borrow?" I ask.

But the party guests love the costume. Several of the other husbands ask me to dance. At first, they are polite about it. Then they get kind of grabby. And when they talk to me, they stare right at my chest. Pigs.

An hour into the party, my daughter pulls out a safety pin. With great flourish, she pops the right breast. Then she pops the left breast.

For this, everyone is thankful.

* * *

It's 10 p.m. and I'm staring into a container of cookie dough ice cream. Only there is no cookie dough left in the cookie dough ice cream. There is only ice cream in the cookie dough ice cream.

This is because some 13-year-old girl stood at the kitchen counter and plucked out all the cookie dough, one sweet spoonful at a time. I don't know this. I sense this, which is about as much evidence as a parent ever needs.

Her: "I want to talk to an attorney."

Me: "Honey, I'm your father. If you're having a problem with cookie dough, you can tell me."

Her: "I want to talk to Johnny Carson."

Me: "Johnnie Cochran?"

Her: "Him, too."

Savvy kid. She just hired a lawyer and a comedian.

Her: "So what if I did eat all the cookie dough, Dad? Would that be so bad?"

She goes on to explain the situation this way. All teenagers have two stomachs – one for real food and one for junk food. So eating cookie dough does not necessarily ruin a teenager's appetite, because she has this other stomach to fill, see, and why am I always picking on her anyway?

I think about this a moment. Then I look down at my own stomach.

Me: "So how many stomachs does a guy like me have?"

Her: "I refuse to answer that."

For that, we are thankful.

* * *

On the other side of the globe, my best friend from college lives in a tent and a Kevlar vest. He is part of the U.S. peacekeeping force in Bosnia-Herzegovina. So instead of spending the holidays with friends and family, he'll spend it with his M-16.

"You'd think that the everyday citizens would just be infuriated with the leaders and want to do all they could to get along," he writes. "But that's not the case."

He talks about the suffering he sees. And the ruin from years of war. The homes and cities, he says, look like something from World War II.

My friend is a member of the Army Reserve. He could have refused the assignment. But he didn't.

For people like this, I am thankful.

* * *

Occasionally, I will drift off to sleep and the little red-haired girl will read a little of the bedtime story on her own before elbowing me awake.

"Dad," she whispers, waking me gently.

So I read a few more pages before drifting back to sleep. While I snore, she reads. It is a pattern I have perfected over 13 years of bedtime stories.

Weary of my catnaps, the 5-year-old cups her hand over my ear and begins to whisper again. It is not so much a whisper as it is a bad kiss. Little kids are always trying to do this, slip in a kiss or a hug when you least expect it.

"Watch it," I warn her.

"Watch what?" she asks.

"You know what I mean," I say sternly. "That kiss. You should know that most of the world's problems started with an innocent kiss. Broken hearts. Bad marriages. Overpopulation. Even wars. They all started with some little kiss."

She is unimpressed by such wisdom. It's clear she will go on with her whisper-kisses no matter what I say.

"Dad," she whispers.

"Yeah?"

"I'm the one who ate the cookie dough," she confesses.

For moments like this, I am thankful.

Happy Thanksgiving.

November 28, 1996

◆ ◆ ◆

On the Tail of a Comet

THE three children are in the back seat of the car, softly singing to the radio and feeling kind of spiritual.

"What if God was one of us ...

"Just a stranger on the bus,

"Trying to make his way home."

All three were snubbed by the Academy, but still they have agreed to come to the back seat of the family car and perform. Which I think shows a lot of class.

"Yeah ... yeah ... yeah, yeah, yeah ...

"What if God was one of us. . . ."

We are driving into the mountains on this cool night – amid the chaparral and the wildflowers – to find a great place to view the Hale-Bopp comet. In just a few minutes, we'll be 6,000 feet up, where it's clear and dark, a quiet place close to God, a place where you can hear yourself sing.

"Yuck," the little boy says. "I smell a skunk."

I explain to the kids that you can't go into nature without smelling a skunk. They're everywhere. So a skunk smell is a good smell really, a sign that you are leaving the city's smog and noise behind.

"I love skunks," the little red-haired girl says.

"That's the spirit," I say.

The kids are well-prepared for the trip, their bellies full of carsickness medication, their brains bursting with visions of the comet. They have already seen it from the house. They have already seen it in the paper. But they have never seen it from a clear mountain vista.

And this car can barely contain the excitement: "Dad, couldn't we just go to a Dodger game?" my older daughter asks. "That's outside. That's nature."

My lovely and patient daughter is concerned because this little comet out-ing is not costing me any money. And as an American teenager, she is deeply suspicious of any activity that is free.

"How can nature be so great if it doesn't have nachos and Dodger Dogs?" she continues.

Such sound reasoning appeals to her younger brother: "Nature should have nachos."

He and his big sister exchange high fives. They have been away from a TV set for almost an hour and are getting a little restless, here in the family car, 4,000 feet up a mountain.

"I think if we just get to the next pass, we'll see the comet," I tell them. "And I assure you, it is a sight you'll never forget."

As the radio reception fades, we drive deeper and deeper into the forest. Pretty soon there are no other cars – just a dad and three kids searching for a comet.

"Hey, Dad, when Hansel and Gretel got lost, weren't they going off to see a comet?" the boy asks.

This immediately gets the attention of the little red-haired girl: "Hansel and Gretel?" She has been leaning against the door, writing her name in the foggy window. But when she hears about Hansel and Gretel, she bolts upright.

"Your brother is just joking," I tell her and scold him.

She doesn't know what to believe now, here in the forest, a good 30 miles from her mommy. She puts her head in her big sister's lap.

"Dad's right. I was just joking," her now-wizened brother assures her.

But the harm has been done. You can't take a 5-year-old into the woods and mention Hansel and Gretel. Not even jokingly. The image will stay with her the entire trip. And well into her dreams.

Finally, the mountains begin to part. A mile or two later, we are over the top, where there is nothing but sky.

As the kids put on their shoes, I spot a parking area and pull over. Except for a guy strumming a guitar, we are alone. In California, there is always some guy with a guitar. Could be the same guy; I'm not sure. But he's everywhere.

The kids grab their flashlights and scramble out of the car, then up a boul-der, trying for the best seat in the house – maybe in all of L.A. – for comet-watching. It's a breathless moment, filled with anticipation and hope.

"Hey, Dad, check out those clouds." The kids are peering up at the sky. They squint. They close one eye; they close the other. Doesn't make any differ-ence, there's still nothing but clouds.

"Yep, those are clouds, all right," the boy says.

The kids are tilted back on the boulder, staring at the sky, waiting for a mir-acle. They have that blank, impassive look you see on men shopping for housewares with their wives.

The little boy is the first to tire of staring at the clouds. To liven things up, he slides off the boulder and pretends to break his leg.

"My tibia!" he yells. "I think I broke my tibia!"

He hops around holding his leg, pretending to be in agony. Understandably, his sisters consider this great entertainment. To them, he's a young Jerry Lewis. Gifted. Possibly a genius. And they begin to laugh like crazy people.

"I totally fractured my tibia!" he yells to the guy with the guitar, who immediately packs up and leaves.

One of the girls passes me a small telescope to look at the clouds. I keep waiting for the clouds to part, like they do in the movies, replaced by that incredible comet.

Five minutes. Ten minutes. Still nothing. By now, the little boy has broken his other tibia and sprained his tongue. The oldest daughter is asleep in the back seat, no doubt dreaming about Dodger Dogs.

Me, I'm still sitting on the boulder, waiting for the comet. Just me, and the little red-haired girl. I'm wondering if it's going to snow. She's wondering if that Hansel and Gretel remark was really true. Every minute or two, she turns around to make sure I'm still here.

"Dad, I like the clouds," she finally says, grabbing my hand. "Thanks for bringing us to see the clouds."

April 13, 1997

CHAPTER FIVE

THE FRIENDS

◆ ◆ ◆

Boys and Grills

HELLO, summer, my old friend. I've come to grill with you again.

Here's the menu: Porterhouse steak. Baked potatoes big as Jay Leno's head. Beer, heavily iced. What else? There is nothing else.

Horseradish, you say? OK, maybe. Every meal needs a vegetable.

"Why Porterville?" my wife asks.

"Why not?" I tell her.

Actually, I'm not sure. My friend, Irv, he's got this butcher shop he likes in Porterville, two hours away. Knows a guy who knows a guy. There are family traditions involved. It's all sort of secretive, like we're headed off to dispose of a body.

"Hey, why Porterville?" I ask Irv one day.

"You'll see," Irv says.

Which makes me think we're headed to some butcher shop/bookie joint/speakeasy. Irv talks of it the way you would a great alehouse. Or a high-stakes poker game.

Knowing Irv, I suspect that this butcher shop offers only a special grade of beef, marinated in garlic and $100 burgundy, then served by butcher's daughters in bikinis. And then, only if you know the password.

"Sure this is legal?" I ask.

"Trust me," Irv says.

So we begin our long drive with thoughts of attorneys and possible jail time.

I've brought a hundred bucks, enough for beef or bail. A hundred bucks, which will get you pretty far in rural Tulare County.

"So why'd you get married?" I ask Irv, who ran off to Vegas recently.

"You know, dude, that's a very interesting story," says Irv, who then begins a very interesting story, about 80 miles long.

Like many love stories, there was magic involved. A bathroom mishap. A childhood friend.

"One night, we just got to talking," he says, as if that explains it all. Which it does.

He tells me about Vegas and the Little Church of the West, where Richard

Gere and Cindy Crawford were married. Judy Garland. Betty Grable. And Irv and Cindy.

"Everything was right," he says.

"Have you ever been with a ballerina?" I ask, fearing for a moment that we will go the entire day without talking about sex or sports.

"You kidding?" he asks. "Back in the '80s . . . "

We reach the butcher shop and load up on steak. Irv gets 10 pounds of porterhouse. I see his 10 pounds of porterhouse, then raise him five T-bones.

He picks up a tri-tip. I pick up a tri-tip. He adds a nice turkey roast for his new bride. I eye the spare ribs.

"This place is great," I tell him, grabbing a bottle of Basque marinade, juiced with three kinds of pepper.

"Look at those steaks," Irv says.

In the back of the shop, one of the butchers is carving 1-inch steaks from the thick end of the short loin. The masterpieces roll off the knife one at a time. Irv and I grunt a little whenever a new steak thumps the table. Touchdown. Home run. Score.

"Comes to $99.83," the cashier says.

Back in the car we go, with 40 pounds of Porterville's finest work stashed in the back. We flee town like bank robbers. The engine growls. Our stomachs grumble.

On the way home, Irv talks about his work. Back in L.A., there's a bunch of stuff happening all at once. A mountain of projects. Nothing special. Just the avalanche of crap that working people deal with on a weekly basis, rewarded by threats of layoffs.

"It's a crap-alanche," Irv explains, then shrugs like it's no big deal.

Irv is a throwback. A raconteur. There are few raconteurs left in the world, guys quick with a story, who know about fly-fishing and quail hunting, whiskey and dogs. In fact, Irv may be the last raconteur. They ought to clone the guy. But carefully.

"So tell me about ballerinas," I tell him, stirring up the conversation for the long ride home.

* * *

"Gotta get it hot," Irv says, as we stand over the grill two hours later.

We are in agreement on the value of heat. First, a steak should be seared on the outside, to seal in the juices. On the inside, it should be medium rare, pink as a puppy's tongue.

"Get that grill white-hot," Irv says.

"How's that?" I ask, stirring the fire.

"Hotter," he says.

Men and fire. There's something about open flames. We sit watching the fire and devolving into cave men. Like werewolves, our bodies are soon completely covered in hair. Our skulls become more oblong, our foreheads more pitched. We're hunched. We're happy.

"How about those Lakers?" I say.

"Ugh," grunts Irv.

When the fire is hot enough, we slap the steaks on my new grill, the one I put together late Christmas Day on the back steps, with the light fading and my wife calling me to dinner. The grill came in a hundred parts, all carefully mislabeled.

I attached the hood while holding a flashlight, my wife and the Christmas star both blinking at me from above.

"Remember all the grills you ever had?" Irv asks.

My first was a hibachi, I tell him. Found it in a college apartment in Des Moines. I would stand out in the snow flipping burgers and dreaming of spring break.

When I got my first job, I splurged on a $5 drugstore grill. My wife and I got a Weber as a wedding gift, then a Kenmore when the kids came along.

Now this new one, which has a little side burner to simmer a pan of onions. With enough grilled onions on top, I'd eat your left shoe. With your left foot still in it.

"To all the grills we've loved before," says Irv, raising a cold beverage as the steaks sizzle, a whisper of summer thoughts in the night.

"To all the grills," I say.

May 9, 2002

◆ ◆ ◆

Man's Best Friend

ON Friday, I take him for a little elective surgery, acknowledging right up front that no surgery should be elective. Either you need it or you don't.

"This wasn't my idea," I explain to the dog.

"I know," he says.

We're standing at the pet clinic, at the front counter. On the other end of the leash is my best and quietest friend. "Lucky" is what we call him. Seemed like a good name at the time.

"Neuter, front desk," the pet clinic clerk calls over the P.A. to the back shop. "Neuter, front desk."

The chilling words echo through the clinic. Lucky looks at me. I look at him. It's an awkward moment. At a time like this, only a dog would still look at you with love in his eyes. Only a dog would be forgiving of such savagery.

"This wasn't my idea," I tell him again.

Dogs and dads, we have a lot in common. We're both hard to live with sometimes. We sneeze too loud and chomp our food, especially the heavy, denser meats. We breathe between bites. We slurp all liquids.

We shed, dogs and dads do. Cats make us crazy – almost psychotic – as do those recent reports that they're cloning kittens. Kittens? Grrrrr, kittens.

Dogs and dads, we're distant cousins really. We'll chase a ball till we drop. If we like something, we will eat it until we become sick. Even in the best of times, our digestive tracts sound like air horns. Some of God's better work, dogs and dads. Simple. Loyal. Strong.

"Neuter, front desk," the pet clinic clerk calls.

"You'll be fine," I tell the dog.

Here's one of those wicked twists life takes: The dog goes in for an ear infection; the vet says maybe it's time for him to be neutered. The cocker spaniel, fresh from his fifth birthday, leaves the pet clinic with an appointment to be "fixed." I think we can all learn from this.

"In what sense, exactly, does he get fixed?" I ask my wife after she makes the appointment.

"Pardon me?"

"Fixed," I say. "I don't think that's the right word."

For in a way, I explain, he'll never be more broken.

"You'll get over it," my wife says. "Both of you."

"Easy for you to say," I tell my wife, obviously a woman.

And I leave Lucky there at the pet clinic, with his feet skating on the cold linoleum floor, his eyes yelling at the pet clinic worker, "Hey, there must be some mistake! You have the wrong dog! Seriously, I'm fine! I'll use a condom!" and the pet clinic worker assuring him that they don't make mistakes like that here, that indeed he's the right dog. That he won't feel a thing.

"He'll die a virgin," I tell my wife when I get home.

"The vet said it'd be best for him," my wife explains.

Exactly how, I don't remember, because I think a chronic virginity is a sad state of affairs, even for a dog.

A chaste life never did anyone much good, leaves you with a cold bed and a cold heart and an unnecessary moral pureness. Watch any of today's more popular movies. Chastity is the devil's work.

"My dog, he'll die a virgin," I complain to my friend Paul.

"You see that Laker game?" Paul asks.

See, no one cares. No one sees the bigger moral implications. This dog, I'd take a bullet for this dog.

Now, he'll never trust me again. Lucky, my loyal friend, the only creature that would ever lick egg yolk from my mustache.

"You should change his name," Paul says.

"To what?"

"To 'Can't Get Lucky.' "

A day later, the dog comes home, without a trace of bitterness. He can't jump, for obvious reasons, and he mostly leaves the stitches alone, doesn't chew at them, for obvious reasons.

He forgives me, mostly, but won't go near the minivan, which he views as an accessory to the crime, an ambulance waiting to carry him back to Dr. Frankenstein's pet clinic.

And in the evening, he rests on the couch with the older daughter and her new boyfriend, home from college for the weekend and watching TV together late into the night. The dog keeps one eye on her. One eye on him.

Always the protector, the dog is the self-appointed sentry for any funny business that might take place there on the couch. He has seen enough movies to know what goes on between America's youth.

Not going to happen. Not on his watch. Especially after all he's just been through. "Make a move," he dares the boyfriend. "I dare you: Make a move."

So how have we rewarded such loyalty? Snip. Snip. And a lot of painkillers. To think that they're cloning cats.

"If they can clone a kitten, they'd better clone a dog," I tell my wife.

"Maybe they could clone Brad Pitt," says my older daughter.

"Maybe they could clone Kobe," says the boy.

No, just my loyal dog, who sleeps on my feet as I write this, his big heart beating against my toes.

March 13, 2002

◆ ◆ ◆

The Invitation

SOMEONE is turning 40.

"Really? Him?" I ask when we get the invite.

"Yes, him," my wife says.

"I thought he was at least 50," I say.

Frankly, the birthday boy looks about 30, but what are you going to say? "Hey, the guy looks great for 40"? You're not going to say that. Once I remarked how good this same guy looked in his driver's license photo. Felt funny about it for days.

So it's going to be a big party, the kind you and your wife prepare to attend a week ahead of time, make sure the kids are set and you don't forget to feed them before you rush out of the door, hard shoes on concrete.

You make extra sure you have the right clothes and that one of you is committed to not drinking too much, a subject of two days of debate.

"You drank last time," she says.

"No, you drank last time," I say.

"No, you drank last time," she says, which is probably true, what with all the pressure I'm under.

Because here's what my wife does for party clothes: She looks in her closet, screams, then slams the closet door, scaring the cat and making the dog all jumpy till he knocks over a vase, which crashes to the floor like a gunshot, setting off car alarms up and down the street and drawing sheriff's cars and helicopters.

"What happened?" one of the kids will ask.

"Your mother just looked in her closet," I'll explain.

"Oh," they'll say, then go back to their e-mail.

Here's what I do for clothes: I look in the closet, then smile.

It's a closet alive with color, shades of brown mostly, the color of footballs and baseball infields, cigars and raccoons. Great color, brown. Wore a brown tux to my wedding. Married a brown-eyed girl. Never went too wrong with brown.

"Dad, you dress," my oldest daughter recently noted, "like a sportswriter from 1985."

"Thanks," I said.

"That wasn't really a compliment," she said.

"That wasn't really a thanks," I said.

It's going to be a big party, fancy as a wedding, held at Casa Del Something in Santa Monica.

Open bar. Big buffet. Women slender as pencils, some of them famous and drop-dead gorgeous.

There'll be fancy hors d'oeuvres on silver platters. Giant shrimp, some of them drop-dead gorgeous. Overlooks the ocean, this party. When a guy makes it all the way to 40, you pull out all the stops.

"I was going to wear my black dress," my wife says.

"You'll look great," I say.

"I can't wear my black dress," she says.

"Of course you can't," I say.

For there is this rumor that one of the other moms might be wearing leather pants. Some of the moms can pull it off, which kind of unnerves the moms who can't.

"Oh, I'll probably just wear my leather pants," the other mom reportedly said a few days before the party, sending shock waves across our oversexed little suburb. Leather? How do you compete with leather? Under their breath, several mothers cursed.

"Whatever you wear will be fine," I tell my wife.

"No, it won't," she says.

"Of course it won't," I say.

"I'm going shopping," she says.

And off she goes shopping with our college-student daughter, who's back in town just to help her mother find something a little hip and sexy.

Remember in the old "Batman" show the sense of doom you felt when the Joker and the Riddler teamed up? That's how I feel watching these two go off shopping for something hip and sexy.

"Where's Mommy going?" asks the little girl.

"Hunting," I say.

They are gone for hours. My wife calls only to ask that we transfer laundry from the washer to the dryer and to be sure the other two kids graduate on time and lead upstanding lives.

"Where's Mom?" the boy wants to know.

"Probably London," I say.

"Shopping?" he asks.

"They'll be home soon," I lie.

Eventually, the shoppers return. They carry their loot in thick, glossy bags, the kind the expensive stores hand out, with soft rope for handles. Heavy bags worth more than most of my shirts. You could make an entire baseball bat with the wood used in one of these bags. You could probably make a chair. Then you'd at least have something to show for it.

"Did you get leather pants?" I ask.

"You don't find leather pants in April," my wife explains.

You don't? I never realized leather was so seasonal. Seems to me you see it all year long.

"When do you find leather?" I ask.

"December," she says.

Of course, December. I've always associated leather with Christmas. Easter is the lingerie holiday. Christmas is for leather.

So we're almost ready to head to the party, where I'll engage in some of the most inane cocktail party chatter you could ever imagine. I'll speculate about what's really in California rolls and borrow the old Woody Allen line on sushi, about not eating anything that's merely unconscious.

At the party, my wife and I will start out together, drift apart, then hook up again at the end, a metaphor for marriage overall. On the way home, she'll sleep a mother's sleep.

"Mom's going to look great," says our older daughter as she pulls blouses from the shopping bags.

"Who?" I say.

"Mom," she says.

"Of course," I say.

April 24, 2002

To Live and Die With Da Bears

RIGHT away, I have two beers on top of two cups of coffee. Mistake. My body is getting a mixed message. Coffee, the stimulant, is telling me to stand up and cheer for my favorite football team. Beer, the relaxant, is telling me to sit down and rest.

Quickly, I come to a compromise where the right half of my body cheers wildly over every play while the left side of my body takes a brief nap. I've always been sort of Siamese in my allegiances.

"I'd better order a cheeseburger," I tell my friend Shaughnessy.

"You'd better order something," Shaughnessy says.

I am in the best of all possible worlds, in a bar on a Saturday afternoon watching a Bears playoff game with a guy named Shaughnessy, who knows all the words to the Bears fight song, one of the finest pieces of music ever penned, containing the best single lyric of all time.

"We'll never forget the way you thrilled the nation,
With the T-formation. ..."

Nobody – not Irving Berlin, not John Lennon – ever wrote a line of song so on point, so full of patriotism and passion.

They also never wrote a song that sounds best sung at the top of your lungs while standing on a bar stool, after 10 or more frosty bottles of happy water.

"Bear down, Chicago Bears,
Let every play clear the way to victory ... "

It's not till we hit age 40 that we really get to know and understand who we are. This I understand: I will always love football.

I don't get to spend every minute of every weekend watching games like I'd like to, but I still love the sport. Love it the way I love Mel Brooks movies, or a stable national currency. Love it the way I love happy water (in moderation, of course).

So I'm here in Burbank with Shaughnessy, a guy who's been known to stand up and sing in public while sober, which is a skill most of us never master.

"Another round?" he sings.

"Sure, why not?" I say.

We're in Burbank, Windy City of the West, in a saloon that draws Bears fans and other assorted Chicago-born scoundrels. Tin Horn Flats, they call it. An elegant piece of plywood on West Magnolia.

We're in the first day of a wondrous January weekend. There are four big playoff games over two days, starting with these Bears against the Philadelphia Eagles, in Soldier Field, football's Mt. Olympus.

Now, up to this point in the season, I've been all right. I haven't overdosed on football. I've consumed it in moderation, mixing it with the kids' soccer and an occasional token chore.

As a result, I've stayed well on the good side of spousal popular opinion, which is never easy. Except for when she told me to shut up on Christmas Day, my wife and I have been able to maintain a pleasant marital truce through the holidays and beyond.

"Good cup of coffee," she gushed the other morning.

"Thanks," I said.

See? I'm on a roll.

So the night before the big game, by candlelight, I tried to explain the next couple of days to her. Saturday, I'd be watching the Bears-Eagles game followed by Raiders-Patriots. On Sunday, Ravens-Steelers, then Packers-Rams.

Over a nice dinner, I explain to my wife how I'm still mostly an NFC guy and always have been. I'm loyal that way. In all ways. Decades pass and I still wear the same pair of loafers.

Loyalty this deep gets to a woman. In the candlelight, I see my wife's eyes moisten. Her fingertips tremble against her wineglass. I see for a moment what we all crave: unbridled love.

"So that's all you're going to do this weekend?" she asks. "Watch football?"

No, I say. On Sunday, I'm going to play football, too. Got a little game of two-hand touch planned with the guys.

"Great," she says. But the subtext is: "Yep, I married an idiot."

Now there are things you will see in a wife's moistened eyes that will bother you in your sleep and your every waking thought. This isn't one of them.

Because I warned her when we were dating 200 years ago that she could do better. "Go," I said. "Find your Lancelot. You're way too good for me."

By the way, my friend Paul used the same psychological double-reverse on his fiancee. "Go," he said. "You deserve better. This is as good as I'll ever get." She stayed, of course. Going on 12 years, the two of them.

So my advice to all you young guys thinking of marriage: First, cast them to the world. Before you marry, offer them their freedom. They will come screaming back forever, with moistened eyes and trembling fingertips. Except, of course, when they don't.

But I digress. We're here to discuss the Chicago Bears, who have special needs of their own. Like an offense, for one.

"This is just like back in the '70s," says Shaughnessy in the second quarter. "They look awful."

The Eagles seem to move the football at will. The Bears respond with random acts of offense. It is turning into a chilly day for our hometown team, even here in beautiful Burbank.

Fortunately, Shaughnessy has lots of stories. Ever met a Shaughnessy who didn't?

"Remember the immortal Bobby Douglass?" he asks, recalling the hapless yet iconic Bears quarterback from a past era. "At least once a game, he'd try to hand the ball off to the referee."

Man, I love football.

January 23, 2002

◆ ◆ ◆

Hollywood Bowl Encore

IT'S Saturday evening at the home of friends. The baked ziti is nearly finished, and there is wine on our wives' lips. Basically, anything could happen.

"So tell us again how you got upside-down in the car," someone asks our friend Debbie.

"I was upside-down?" Debbie asks.

Flash back to a week earlier. The Hollywood Bowl.

James Taylor is in concert. For almost three hours he sings us lullabies in night air that is dry and cool as a virgin's kiss.

Just yesterday morning, they let me know you were gone,
Suzanne, the plans they made put an end to you.

Taylor stands up on stage with 25% of the hair he once had, one of rock's last remaining troubadours, singing his songs of the past and painting pictures in the dark.

We sit there with 25% of the hair we once had, hanging on to his every word.

"We love you, James!" a fan shouts between songs.

"Thank you, sir," Taylor answers dryly.

Taylor's voice is better than ever – choirboy clear, as if filtered through stained glass.

He's supported by six musicians and 18,000 backup singers, a sold-out Hollywood Bowl audience insistent on helping him perform.

Many merely lip-sync the words to his classic songs. Others are less considerate. Some fans sing louder than Taylor himself.

"The guy sitting behind us, he was singing so loud," says a friend we run into at intermission.

"Come sit with us," we offer.

"Seriously?"

"Sure, there's plenty of room," I say.

Now, if you've ever been in a box at the Hollywood Bowl, you know there isn't exactly plenty of room.

It's like a game of Twister, only more intimate, and your chances of contracting a cold or falling in love are pretty good, even if you're not looking for illness or love, which share many of the same awful symptoms.

A Hollywood Bowl box is a phone booth really, with four to six chairs wedged inside. When my wife breathes in, I breathe out. If one person in our group itches, we all have to scratch. Women have gotten pregnant in the Hollywood Bowl just reaching for the brie.

"You have enough room there?" someone asks.

"Oh, sure."

So our friends Joel and Mona crawl in, bringing our group to six, maximum occupancy.

As Taylor takes a long halftime break, the six of us share some dessert and finish each other's laughs.

"We're seeing who can spot the hottest celebrity," I tell Joel.

"OK, we'll play," he says.

Debbie's husband spots Jamie Lee Curtis. Joel tops him with Helen Hunt.

"Look over there," I say.

"Where?"

"Courteney Cox," I say.

"Where?"

"Or maybe it's Howard Stern," I say.

Then the second half begins.

> In my mind I'm goin' to Carolina,
> Can't you see the sunshine,
> Can't you just feel the moonshine,
> Ain't it just like a friend of mine to hit me from behind,
> Yes, I'm going to Carolina in my mind.

James Taylor sings and talks, talks and sings. He introduces the musicians and singers, many of whom have been with him for years.

The crowd sits politely through an acoustic set, blood pressure medication and Chardonnay mingling in our veins.

Believe it or not, you're not supposed to bring bottles of wine into the Bowl anymore. So we sneak it in. In our veins.

> Take to the highway won't you lend me your name,
> Your way and my way seem to be one and the same.

Four encores. That's right, four, if my math is correct.

Taylor sings an encore, then leaves for five minutes. Comes out, sings another short ditty, then leaves for five more minutes.

"Sing the whole song!" someone in our box yells after the third quick encore.

Taylor ends the evening with "Sweet Baby James," his signature song, sending everyone to the cars happy and a little sad.

Goodnight, you moonlight ladies,
Rockabye, sweet baby James,
Deep green and blues are the colors I choose,
Won't you let me go down in my dreams,
Yes, and rockabye sweet baby James.

We cow-walk out of the amphitheater with 18,000 other people, bumping elbows and flanks as we sway down the hill toward our cars.

"Another couple of days, we'll be outta here," I say optimistically when we reach the minivan.

"Here, let's sit in the back," my wife says, opening the tailgate.

At the Bowl, no one leaves right away. Cars are parked bumper-to-bumper-to-bumper.

Weeks pass, and no one moves. No one can leave till the car in front or to the side leaves. Sometimes it takes 30 minutes. Other times, hours or weeks.

Which I think is how our friend Debbie wound up upside-down in the back of the minivan at midnight, with us circled around laughing and eating Trader Joe's cheese. An impromptu tailgate party.

"Hey, Debbie, how'd you get upside-down?" her husband yells.

"I'm upside-down?" she asks.

A week later, we finish the baked ziti and relive the concert. With today's ticket prices, we have to go twice to justify the expense. First, in person. Then, a week later, in our best friends' home.

"We should go to more concerts," Debbie says.

"Sure, when?" my wife asks.

There is wine on the wives' lips again. Basically, anything could happen. And usually doesn't.

"How'd we get home that night anyway?" Debbie says, an age-old question we rarely get to ask anymore.

"Very carefully," someone answers.

And rockabye sweet baby James.

October 17, 2001

◆ ◆ ◆

Buddy-Buddy

THE dog and I are watching TV, one of those real-life cop shows where they arrest real people and dish out real justice.

In this segment, the police are pursuing a suspect under a house. Instead of crawling under the house themselves, the cops send in the police dogs, who really seem to enjoy chasing bad guys under houses.

"One of these days," I tell my cocker spaniel, "I'm taking you on a police raid."

This fills the fluffy little dog with excitement. He's watched a lot of these cop shows, seen a lot of police raids, but he's never seen a cocker spaniel chase a suspect under a house.

"Yep," I tell him, "I think the police could use a cocker spaniel like you."

The dog looks at me. This really pumps him up, hearing that one day he could become a police dog. He is so grateful, he is almost in tears.

"Hey, police dogs don't cry," I warn him.

Two years ago, the dog was a reject, an outcast puppy in need of a home. Neighbors offered him to us when he "didn't quite work out."

"We don't really need a dog," I told my wife at the time.

"Everybody needs a dog," she said.

In weeks, the dog and I became best buddies. Not just friends, but buddies, the kind of pals who can laugh about anything, especially each other.

And I soon found that he believes everything I say. One day I convince him I'm a cop. The next day, a neurosurgeon. He even believes I once played fullback for the Green Bay Packers.

"That Lombardi was a heck of a coach," I tell him. "And a darned good dancer as well."

He loves it when I tell stories about my football career. Can't get enough of them. He sits on my lap and looks up at me, encouraging me to tell him more.

"Really enjoyed the NFL," I tell him. "Might even make a comeback."

The dog's eyes get real big when I mention comeback. He'd like to see me play, would love to sit right here on the couch on Sunday afternoons and watch his 155-pound owner run the ball up the middle against the Chicago Bears, dragging gigantic defenders into the end zone.

"Dad, you spend too much time with that dog," my lovely and patient oldest daughter says, shaking her head in disbelief. "You treat him like ... like a person."

My daughter is probably right. I do spend a lot of time with the dog. He's good company. Everything I do seems to interest him. When I stir my coffee he waits and watches, his head going round and round with each rotation of the spoon. One day he spent four hours just watching me make soup.

"This dog's grateful for every little thing," I tell her.

"And I'm not?" she asks.

There is a long pause. I try to think how to phrase my response. She's a good daughter. Lovely. Patient. And, generally, pretty darned grateful.

"Dad?"

"You're grateful," I say. "But not as grateful as he is."

The cocker spaniel is grateful in ways that kids seldom think of. He's grateful that there's always food in the house. He's grateful when the furnace kicks on in the middle of a chilly night. He's grateful when I accidentally drop a piece of bacon off the counter.

"I'm grateful, too," says the little red-haired girl.

"Me, too," says her brother.

Suddenly, everybody in the house is grateful. I guess that's all you have to do sometimes is bring up the word "grateful," and sure enough, they'll all line up and nod their little heads.

"Yep, we're grateful," they'll say.

"I know you're all grateful," I assure them. "Everybody here is grateful. And I'm grateful for it."

As this fine display of gratitude comes to a close, I go to the closet and grab my old sweater.

The dog knows this is his cue, that when I grab my old sweater, it's time for our nightly walk, a stroll up the road, where I will entertain him with stories of cop life and the difficulties of performing an arterial bypass.

He stands by the door like a live mop, all jumpy and wiggly, doing a tap dance on the tile floor, hoping we're on our way to catch our first criminal.

"Want to come along?" I ask my patient and lovely oldest daughter.

"I don't know," she says.

"Oh, come on," I say. "We might catch a criminal."

The teenager looks at me. Then down at the dog. Apparently, the two of us look like a comedy act. Or at least a couple of guys in need of some decent company.

"I'll get my coat," she says.

March 4, 1998

◆ ◆ ◆

The Bunco Players

GENERALLY, a little economic chaos is good for a family. It keeps you from focusing on each other's various personal shortcomings and keeps the eye always on the prize. The mortgage payment at the end of the month. A college education.

"You know, tonight I've got bunco," my wife tells me at breakfast.

"Again?" I ask.

Remember how men used to get together for poker? Now the wives are getting together for these bunco games, where they gather in someone's home to gamble a little, guzzle wine and joke about their sex lives. At least that's what the husbands assume they're doing. There could be more to bunco, but I doubt it.

The wives could be using these meetings to plot to take over the White

House or reorganize the U.N. They could be talking Fed policy.

Or, generous as they are, these bunco girls could be figuring out how to make their husbands happier and more fulfilled.

They could be planning lavish weekends away with their husbands to reward us for taking a greater role in raising the kids. For all the little things we do that our dads didn't. The dishes. The diapers. Algebra.

But I doubt it.

"Where's Mom?" the little girl asks.

"Bunco," I say.

"Who's going to help me with my homework?"

"Call your sister," I say.

Women. For a while, they had us thinking they were better than us, more dedicated and reliable, some of them, in fact, quite perfect.

Now we're learning that women have their weaknesses, too.

They're quick to make fun of us with our Final Four brackets, yet they're all googly-eyed over those silly Oscar ballots.

They used to scold us over poker nights. Now they have this bunco, which apparently is a simple dice game where you rotate from table to table, wine sloshing everywhere, money exchanging hands. Laughter. Camaraderie.

At the end of the evening, the winner leaves with enough cash for decent pair of shoes.

As they gamble these nights away, dark clouds gather over our once-proud land. Dishes pile up. Homework, too. The republic may never recover.

In the morning, most everyone has a headache.

"What time did you get home?" I ask.

"Why?"

"Just curious."

"Eleven," she says, stirring her coffee, looking into it for answers.

"On a school night?" I ask.

"Yes, on a school night," says bunco girl.

March is the money month. Everywhere you look there's some school fundraiser or a half-dozen silent auctions. At the spring fair, a silent auction. At the PTA dinner, yet another.

Eventually, all transactions will be made through silent auctions. Need a new car? Sign that list over there. Going to Greece? Try to outbid Bob and Lynda. You readers turn to this space every week to find out what's really going on in America, and I'm here to tell you that if these silent auctions don't ruin us as a nation, bunco will.

"I never knew Charlotte was so much fun," my wife says, recalling some bunco pal.

"I wouldn't know," I say.

Beware these Ides of March. The tax man cometh. Bunco is sweeping the land. There are all those silent auctions. Even those Nixon girls are haggling over money. Secret bunco junkies, probably.

Then last week, the Girl Scout cookie cash comes due. As always, we are short about 60 bucks.

What happens, usually, is that the Girl Scout cookie money comes in, and we tap into the envelope for emergency cash for school or dinner then wind up writing a check to cover the difference.

It's check-kiting at its worst, the kind of monetary policy favored by Third World dictators. Orange County once invested this way. Enron, too.

"I hope," I warn my wife, "that you didn't use Girl Scout money for bunco."

"Mighta," she says without remorse.

Evidently, there's a reason those Thin Mints look like poker chips. One day, they may replace cash.

"At school, guess who's winning their NCAA bracket?" the boy asks.

"Your mom?"

"No, me," he says.

Oh mother, where art thou? How come all of a sudden I feel like Hamlet?

"Talked to the tax guy today," my wife says.

"And?"

"He says tennis lessons count as day care," she says.

"In Brazil?"

"No, here," she says.

Beware the wives of March.

March 20, 2002

◆ ◆ ◆

When Bad Players Happen to Good Games

"Football is a kids' game, invented to give a lot of people a lot of fun."
　　　　　—Joe Kapp, former quarterback

"What I miss most is the violence."
　　　　　—Dick Butkus, former linebacker

THE glory of touch football is that it's a game that never evolves – no instant replay, no domed stadiums – just a bunch of domed dads out on a chilly Sunday, trying to keep middle age at bay and stay healthy and desirable for our wives.

Because let me tell you a little secret about today's wives: They're lovely and caring. But let yourself go a little and they'll dump you like a load of shirts. Just ask Gino.

"She dumped me again," Gino told me one night at the local steak place.

"She can't dump you," I say. "You're her husband."

Gino explains that some women become so accustomed to dumping us that by the time they marry, it's imprinted on the right side of their female cortex, just behind their pretty foreheads. To them, dumping becomes second nature. Like blinking or buying on credit.

"I'm constantly trying to win her back," says Gino.

Which is why we're out here playing touch football on Sunday afternoon, a bunch of aging Huck Finns trying to hang on to our boyhoods and our marriages, an improbable goal.

"You, run a slant," Hank says, designing a play in the huddle.

"You, go long," he tells someone else.

"Me?"

"Hook-and-go," he says.

Then we all clap our hands and line up for the next thrilling play. Hank likes when we clap our hands after huddles. Shows we're a unit.

And off I go, running my hook-and-go pattern, which I make up as I run it, sort of the way I make soup.

"What was that?" Hank says when I come back to the huddle.

"Hook-and-go," I gasp.

"Right," he says.

Lately, our games have become a little chaotic. We have had such huge turnouts – eight to 10 players per team, many of them our sons and daughters – that the plays unfold with the skill and timing of a badly botched convenience store holdup.

Now, I admire chaos in a sporting event. Too much precision, and you lose the fans. A soulless precision is the NFL's worst enemy. That and those awful indoor stadiums. Tombs, really. Give me games in the snow and the slop. Give me touch football.

"What happened there?" I ask Hank after eight of our 10 receivers collide on a crossing pattern.

"Not a clue," Hank growls.

By the second quarter, I have taken to inventing my own pass patterns and then naming them after people I admire.

On short yardage, I run something called the Jayne Mansfield. Long yardage, the Loni Anderson, a big loop followed by another big loop, followed by big hair.

"What's he doing?" I can hear the free safety ask.

"Heck if I know," the cornerback says, and they turn their attention to players younger and more dangerous.

I used to be a player. At 19, I could catch a jellybean dropped from a fighter jet. At 25, I was quick as a stolen kiss.

Now, two decades later, I have almost no game left. So I make the most of what I have, running pass routes shaped like chesty actresses of yesteryear. Barbara Eden. Adrienne Barbeau.

"How'd he get so open?" I hear Eisen ask.

"Who cares?" Burlison says.

One week, we made the mistake of putting Eisen and Burlison, both lawyers, on the same team. Being attorneys, they won every rule dispute by sheer stubbornness.

At one point, they issued a restraining order against our nose tackle, the little red-haired girl, who would patiently count "one Mississippi, two Mississippi, three Mississippi," then scamper like a field mouse at their hairy lawyer legs.

Later, in a crucial series, the two lawyers refused to honor our call for a timeout, acting as if they were in court and couldn't hear the other attorney objecting.

"Timeout!" I screamed about four times, nearly pulling a hamstring in my tongue.

"Huh?" said Burlison.

"Hike," said Eisen.

"Timeout!" I screamed again.

My advice: When forming teams for touch football, don't put all the lawyers on the same team. Too competitive. Too tactical.

My other advice: Always stretch. In football, and in life, be sure to stretch. Stretch before the game. Stretch during the game. Stretch in the ambulance on the way to the hospital.

Because once you've pulled a muscle, in your tongue or in your leg, it is pulled forever. Sure, it'll heal a little, but only enough to make you think you're fine again.

Then snap. Ouch. Down you'll go. The sniper shot you never hear.

"How many groin muscles do we have?" Eisen asks.

"Me? Hundreds," I say.

"I just pulled them all," he says.

The dads – some pushing 40, others 50 – play every down as if it's our very last.

And the kids, ranging in age from 10 to 16, play every down as if it's a skit for a fifth-grade play, laughing in key moments and mugging for the crowd. The kids' basic philosophy of football is that if it makes someone laugh, it's a good play.

"We done yet?" one of the dads mumbles after an hour.

"We were done 20 years ago," Ulf says.

Late in the game, the dads begin to lose all remaining body heat out of the tops of our heads, a sort of chimney effect I can't explain.

The kids, meanwhile, get fresher and happier with every play. Most are video game kids, unaccustomed to fresh air and sunlight. Many are out of doors for the very first time. Like Huck Finn, they seem to take to it.

"It's sort of nice to get out of the house," a teenager says on a perfectly rainy and sloppy Sunday.

Touchdown.

January 30, 2002

◆ ◆ ◆

The Dinner Party

HERE we are hosting our first dinner party of the new century, a small but elegant affair featuring candlelight and boneless chicken breasts and lots of sophisticated, adult conversation.

"Nice breasts," my friend Hank says, leering at the chicken.

"Vons," I say.

"Are they real?" Martha asks.

"They're real," says Hank, prodding them with a fork.

It's one of those intimate dinner parties, just ourselves and one other couple. The adults talk in the kitchen. The children go to war at the far end of the house, which isn't very far at all.

"How many kids do you have again?" I ask Hank.

"Forty," he says.

"Sounds like more," I say.

"Sounds like a hundred," says his wife, Martha.

Every now and then, we hear the dull thud of a kid's head hitting a closet door or the yelp of someone being tossed around like a pillow. Nice sounds. Frightening sounds. Under different circumstances, the sort of happy party sounds that precede a murder.

"Our kids play well together," I say.

"I think I hear a siren," Hank says.

"Settle down back there," I yell.

Like a lot of elegant L.A. dinner parties, we start in the kitchen with margaritas and a bottle of wine. Martha offers to crush the ice with a metal mallet. Hank mixes the drinks. Then we all head to the bathroom.

In the bathroom, we close the door so the kids can't find us, then we admire the grout.

It is like an old episode of "Knots Landing" – four adults in an L.A. bathroom, drinking and relaxing. Except that we are talking about tile and grout.

"Why did it crack like that?" Hank asks.

"I don't know," I say.

"Could've been too dry," he says.

"In the shower, it held up fine," I say.

"These are nice towel bars," Martha says.

We like the way our voices sound in the bathroom. For 10 minutes, we hang around the tub and discuss how well the brass faucet is holding up, not getting all brown the way brass often does.

"This is going well," I whisper to my wife, relieved at how the dinner party is turning out.

"Don't jinx it," she says.

Moving to the patio, we admire the food cooking on the barbecue and breathe in the rich, thick smoke of the grill.

We revel in the open flames, Hank and I. The more the fire flares up, the happier we get, the flames reflecting off the margarita glasses and our wives' teeth and jewelry.

"Want to eat outside?" my wife asks.

"Sure," somebody says.

It has been the mildest of winters, good for barbecues and Saturday night dinner parties like this one, where we can sit outside in the sweaters we got for Christmas and savor the garlic and the smoke.

Mostly, we just talk. It's the kind of adult conversation we can never get enough of – talk about the kids and schools and the auto show and how Marino should retire, better now than later, when he might be forced to limp away from football in disgrace.

We talk about movies and orthodontics and soccer games that ended badly.

HMOs and kitchen renovations and dot-coms.

"It's like a gold rush," I say as we discuss the Internet.

"Or a house of cards," Hank says.

What we don't talk about is politics. Almost no one I know is talking about politics. I guess everyone has better things to discuss. Or they're tired of it all.

In any case, politics has become almost invisible now. Which, in good times like these, is probably what politics should be. Invisible.

"Do you smell something burning?" my wife asks.

"I don't know," Martha says.

"I think I smell something burning," she says, her nose to the air like a mother deer.

"It's the candles," Hank says.

"It's the grill," I say.

"No, really, I smell something else burning," my wife says.

Like many women, my wife has an extraordinary sense of smell. She is always smelling something burning. At a ballgame. At the mall. At our wedding.

She smells refinery fires in Texas, truck blazes in Maine. A tugboat catches fire on the Mississippi River, she's the first to notice. It's a gift, really, this sense of smell.

"I smell something too," Martha says.

"It's the grill," Hank says.

"I think she smells the rain forests," I say.

And that's how our first dinner party of the 21st century goes, much like dinner parties of the past, scented with barbecue smoke and just enough adult conversation to keep us going, to let us know that our problems are their problems and vice versa – that there are no new problems, just new parents.

On the other side of the house, a kid screams. A cat cusses. Heavy footsteps. Then silence. Somewhere, a bunch of kids are huddled together, coming up with an excuse.

"Our kids play so well together," I say.

"I think something's burning," my wife says.

"Wanna go look at the grout again?" Hank asks.

"Sure," I say.

January 19, 2000

◆ ◆ ◆

A Day at the Beach

IT'S a little chilly when I awaken, cooler than usual for so early in September, and I stand barefoot for a moment in the spot where the dog slept, where it is warm on the rug, thinking that I need to get a warmer house or a bigger dog.

"Are we going to the beach?" my older daughter asks.

"Sure," I say.

"Because it's kind of cold," she says.

"Come stand over here," I say.

So we stand together in the warm spot for a few minutes, then look outside at the gray sky, which threatens to ruin our holiday weekend. Just our luck: global cooling.

Because this was going to be a big beach day, the last beach day of the year, with food and football and significant idle time, which is what Labor Day weekend is about. Idle time. The last idle time of the year, before school and soccer and all that other stuff kicks in.

"We really going to the beach?" asks a little girl, stepping from the bedroom and rubbing her face awake.

"Sure," I say.

"My feet are cold," she says.

"Stand over here," her big sister says.

For breakfast, they have doughnuts and sliced kiwi; the kiwi they eat with their fingers. The doughnuts they eat with a fork.

Then we pile into the car and head toward Laguna. At 11 a.m., several other vehicles still have their headlights on.

"It's, like, foggy out, Dad," the boy says.

"I don't see any fog," I tell them.

"It's everywhere, Dad," my lovely and patient older daughter points out.

"It's just a little fog," I say.

And we reach the beach, where the fog lifts to expose an ocean that is slate gray and a sky that's in turmoil. For a moment, the kids think I have brought them to watch a hurricane.

"I think I see a water spout," my older daughter says.

"I think I see the sun," I say.

Sure enough, the sky eventually brightens and the sand begins to warm.

The kids splash off into the ocean, jumping up when the waves arrive, then ducking under, till a wave flips them backward and up onto the beach.

Pretty soon, other families arrive. Then there is a football game, dads against the kids, one of those gridiron mismatches you see early in the season like this. An easy first game against a smaller opponent. Next week, the dads play Penn State.

"Let's go in the water," someone yells, and both teams head for the surf, diving into the water after their tough game, rinsing off the sand and the sweat, floating on Boogie boards and tossing the football some more, turning the ocean into testosterone soup.

"My head's like an aquarium," brags the boy after a few minutes.

"Mine, too," I say.

For 45 minutes, the dads and boys rest and roll atop the ocean, seawater going in their ears, seawater going out. Sea creatures going in their ears. Sea creatures going out.

Zooplankton. Small crustaceans. Maybe a jellyfish or two. Now and then, a baby shark.

So we float a little longer, ride a few waves, then float some more, thinking about guy stuff – point spreads and processor speeds and Daryl Hannah. To this day, a lot of guys cannot go near an ocean without thinking of Daryl Hannah. Just for a moment, she splashes in our heads.

"Let's eat," someone says, so we crawl ashore and fire up the tiny grill and slap on a hundred hot dogs, take them off, then slap on a hundred more.

And as the sun fades and the radio plays, we bid so long to the beach, the place where summer is at its best. A festival, really. The last bacchanal before fall.

Down by the water, two older revelers are walking, holding hands. As we watch quietly, they share a kiss.

"Ever see grandparents kiss?" I ask the little girl.

"No," she says.

"It's a beautiful thing," I tell her.

"It is?" she asks.

"Especially at the beach," I say. "If I'm ever a grandparent, I'm going to kiss like crazy."

"You are?" she asks.

"I'm planning on it," I say.

She thinks about this a moment. A wave comes in, nearly stealing our cooler.

"You're going to kiss Mom?" asks the little girl.

"Almost exclusively," I say.

"That's disgusting, Dad," says my older daughter.

"Yeah, Dad, I'm trying to eat," says the boy.

"I'm going to kiss like crazy," I whisper to the little girl.

"Me, too," she says.

September 8, 1999

THE GUY

◆ ◆ ◆

Marathon in a Minivan

SCENES from a family car trip:

DAY 1: The open road. A full tank of gas. Kids in the back seat. Maps on Mom's lap. I zero out the odometer. I zero out the kids. Out of the garage we roar, as if leaving the Bat Cave. The pace car for summer vacation.

"Dad, is it hard to drive?" the little girl asks.

"Not really," I say.

"Because you make it look so easy," she says.

"Here, have a dollar," I say.

By noon, we are in the land where you pump first, then pay, a small token of trust that encourages us to continue. Gas is 20 cents cheaper. You can see the sky.

In the back seat, it smells like a garden party. I'm pretty sure there are cut flowers.

DAY 2: The open road. A full tank of gas. Kids in the back seat. Maps missing.

"I think you're sitting on them," my wife says.

"They'll be safe there," I say.

In Denver, my wife does that little thing with her hands that she does when she thinks I'm not slowing down soon enough for traffic stopped ahead. Like someone shaking out a match. Like someone watching a no-hitter.

"Thanks for the help," I say.

"No sweat," she says.

"I spilled Orange Crush in my shoe," the boy says.

"I want Orange Crush in my shoe," the little girl says.

By 4 p.m., the back seat smells like a frat party. I'm pretty sure there is beer.

DAY 3: The open road. A full tank of gas. Tic Tacs rattling in all the ashtrays. Underwear flapping from a window.

"Mom, what's a common-law marriage?" the boy asks.

His mother explains common-law marriages.

"See, we're married," the boy tells his little sister, which makes the little girl break into tears. I don't know if she's happy or sad. As with most brides, it's hard to tell.

"Get a lawyer," her older sister suggests.

"OK," says the little girl.

To pass the time, the kids make signs with Magic Markers and hold them up to passing truckers.

"Just married," one sign says.

"Honk if you're bored," another says.

"Have you seen my duck?" asks another.

By 4 p.m., the back seat smells like boiled socks. And a type of cheese I cannot at first identify.

"Car-trip cheese," I finally say to my wife.

"Huh?" she says.

"Never mind," I say.

DAY 4: The open road. A full tank of gas. After breakfast, my wife calls me "Dagwood," then threatens to leave me for the mini-mart attendant at the Shell.

"He seemed so nice," my wife says as we pull away.

"Dad, if she goes, we're staying with you," the boy says.

"No, we're not," says the little girl.

"That's your choice," I tell them.

For lunch, we stop in the little Iowa town where Buffalo Bill was born.

"Wanna see the Buffalo Bill museum?" I ask.

"Yes!" the little girl screams.

"Dad, don't let this get any worse," my older daughter says.

"That clerk, he seemed so nice," my wife says.

"My leg is bleeding," says the boy.

By 4 p.m., the back seat smells like a zoo. I think there's a monkey loose.

And in the nick of time, we arrive in Chicago, proudly wearing the dirt of eight dusty states.

The kids tumble from the car, then grunt when their grandmother hugs them hard. For several minutes, they struggle to get their breath back.

"She hugs good," says the little girl, staggering toward the house.

The Midwest is bigger than we remember it. Friendly. The sort of place where presidents are born.

For eight days, the children run rampant across northern Illinois, swimming and fishing and throwing rocks in rivers. They chase their cousins. They eat watermelon with their noses and chins.

When they run out of things to do, they sit on the back porch and count their mosquito bites, as if comparing souvenirs.

"I've got 12," one says.

"I've got 15," says another.

"That's a nipple," one explains.

"No it's not."

"Let's not talk about nipples," I say.

On the ninth day, we load up the car. The kids climb back aboard, three car-trip cosmonauts, ready for another mission.

"My face is bleeding," says the boy.

"That's Grandma's lipstick," his older sister explains.

"She kisses good," the little girl says.

The car sputters as we pull out of the driveway, as if we left a sparkplug in the garage.

"Bye, Grandma!" they yell, waving out the back window.

Somehow, the sputtering minivan keeps going, pointed back across the prairie.

"I can't believe it," my wife says.

"What?" I say.

"It's over," she says sadly.

"Not yet," I say.

The open road. A full tank of gas. Two thousand miles till home.

August 25, 1999

◆ ◆ ◆

Homeward Bound

SOMEWHERE IN CENTRAL NEBRASKA – Bonnie and Clyde used to take car trips like this, long wonderful drives across the country, stopping occasionally to use the restroom and hold up a bank or a Dairy Queen, then climbing back in the car and licking each other's ears. Romantic car trips, a hundred cop cars screaming in pursuit.

"Wanna rob a liquor store?" I ask my wife as we speed down the prairie highway.

"Maybe after lunch," she says, curling up with the TripTiks.

You try to make a family car trip a little fun, and this is what you get. A sensible answer. A car trip snooze.

So onward I drive, passing little towns full of liquor stores and banks and Dairy Queens, regretting what we missed. By Utah, we could've been rich.

"Dad, what are you doing?" asks a little girl in the back seat.

"I'm just hallucinating," I say.

"OK," she says, going back to sleep.

It's been a long car trip, 3,000 miles of open road and corn. A thousand horses. A trillion cows. No farmers.

We will pass hundreds and hundreds of farms on our eight-state journey and never see a single farmer in the fields. Maybe they work at night. Maybe they're in Tahoe.

"What are you doing now?" the little girl asks 20 minutes later.

"Still hallucinating," I say.

"That's good, Dad," the little girl says.

"Yeah, just what you want in a driver," grumbles my lovely and patient older daughter.

* * *

We're headed home, which always changes the mood of a car trip, dampens the energy, saps its strength.

For 3,000 miles now, the kids have had to look at the back of my neck. It's a nice neck, but after a few thousand miles, it becomes less and less interesting.

So they study my ears, the way my sunglasses curve around the top of them, the way the sunlight dances on the plastic.

Then they study my neck again. Neck. Ears. Neck. Like that, for 3,000 miles. All in all, they've handled this excitement very well.

"Are we stopping?" the little girl asks.

"No, don't stop," says the boy.

"Stop," says the little girl.

"Don't stop," says the boy.

More than anything, they'll remember the food. Mexican food in Iowa. Cajun in Colorado. The Chinese joint in Nebraska that served a fine plate of snow peas and shrimp, the shrimp seemingly shrink-wrapped in their own skins. Platte River shrimp. Big as a baby's thumb.

"Good steak," says the boy, gnawing as if on a Band-Aid.

"That's a shrimp," I say.

"Real chewy," he says.

"The best shrimp always are," I tell him.

So they cut the little shrimp into tiny pieces, then pour on steak sauce and savor every rubbery bite. Because they know they don't get shrimp very often. Only in Nebraska, when Dad's wallet is filled with 50s and Mom's drinking some blue umbrella drink and talking about her college days. Nebraska, they've found, is a seafood lover's paradise.

"How about some lobster?" my older daughter asks.

"Eat your shrimp," I say.

* * *

Now we're gliding home, up through the Rockies on a hot afternoon, with the minivan's four cylinders chattering like chipmunks.

Every 90 seconds, I look down at the heat gauge, which seems never to move. Cool rains. Hot mountains, the needle never moves. Painted on, probably. Like on a toddler's play car.

"What are you looking at?" my wife asks.

"Nothing," I say.

"You're looking at something," she says.

"The altimeter," I say.

"The what?"

"Nothing."

And down the Rockies we go, then into Utah, where my older daughter takes the wheel – the world's newest driver. For an hour, everything I cherish is at her slender fingertips.

"Remember, I love this car," I tell her as she zooms along the interstate.

"Sure, Dad," she says.

At one point we come around the side of a mountain to discover a small herd of deer, maybe a dozen, standing inches from the interstate, nibbling on dry grass and a McDonald's bag.

"That could've been dangerous," my daughter says, looking at the animals in her mirror.

"You did fine," I say.

"Wow," she whispers under her breath.

In Las Vegas, I take back the wheel – for Interstate 15, the world's longest roller-coaster, bumper-to-bumper traffic at 70 mph, Las Vegas to San Bernardino.

A great way to end a long car trip, the I-15, with a final death-defying drop through the Cajon Pass on a Sunday afternoon, trucks on three sides, their brakes cooking on the steep grade.

"We're almost home," says the boy.

"We're home?" asks the little girl.

"Almost," says the boy.

"What are you looking at, Dad?" asks my older daughter.

"The altimeter," I say.

And finally, like Bonnie and Clyde, our glamorous cross-country trip comes to a sudden close, the car's grill baked with bugs, me just baked.

I get out of the car stiff and slow, pushing the palm of my hand against my lower back the way old men and pregnant women do, trying to straighten up.

"Who left the Silly Putty on the back seat?" I ask.

"That's not Silly Putty, Dad," the boy says.

"Yeah, that's not Silly Putty," the little girl says.

"It looks like Silly Putty," I say.

"Well, it's not," says the boy.

"Welcome home, honey," my wife says, patting me on the shoulder.

"We're home?" I ask.

"Yeah, we're home," she says.

September 1, 1999

♦ ♦ ♦

Random Thoughts

A selection of assorted observations from "The Guy Chronicles":

• Youth is wasted on the young.

• Wealth is wasted on the rich.

• France is wasted on the French.

• Joan Rivers' New York accent gets thicker every year.

• So does her makeup.

• If Wilbur and Orville Wright could've foreseen LAX, they never would have attempted flight.

• If you help a friend, you help yourself.

• Every Friday is a good Friday.

• All food is comfort food.

• I always want fries with that.

• Best nut: the cashew.

• Best sedative: a good dog.

• The word "jewelry" always looks misspelled.

• How can there be no "r" in the word "colonel"?

• Quote of the day: "The time you enjoy wasting is not wasted time."

(Bertrand Russell)

• Extension cords are always 2 feet too short.

- Today's NFL coaches look too much like golfers.

- In the long run, companies concerned only about their stock price are doomed to fail.

- The team with the better quarterback almost always wins.

- All drives are hard drives.

- All money is hard money.

- Everyone looks better by candlelight.

- There is no better alarm clock than a pan of simmering bacon.

- Common sense isn't all that common.

- Neither is horse sense nor common decency.

- I've never roasted chestnuts on an open fire. And I don't know any one who has.

- In general, people don't bake enough.

- The best pie: blueberry.

- Once a day, you should lose your breath.

- School boards are more important than city councils.

- Beer can never be too cold.

- Rock 'n' roll has never been worse.

- Cars have never been more reliable.

- $50 bills should be a different color – like in Monopoly.

- Driver's tests are too easy.

- Larry Gelbart and Carl Reiner should run a television network.

- Shania Twain should have her own Sunday night variety show.

- The college football season ends too soon.

- Remember when a Timex watch was all the personal technology you needed?

- Favorite line from the late Steve Allen (from his early days as a disc jockey): "I have the final score for you on the big game between Harvard and William & Mary. It is: Harvard 14, William 12, Mary 6."

- Basically, there are no shortcuts.

- Most of the best things in life are really, really expensive.

- If you have children, you have everything.

◆ ◆ ◆

Let There Be Lights

FOR Christmas, I bought her pearls. Plastic pearls. Ten bucks a box.

"Hand me that next string," I tell the boy.

"This one?" he asks.

"Yeah, that one."

We string them along the rain gutter, hanging them from little hooks that I slip over the gutter's lip. Every few feet, I place a hook. From below, the boy feeds me the tiny pearl-like lights.

"These icicle lights are going to look great," says the boy.

"Right," I say.

For years, we have strung lights along the rain gutters. This year, those lights suddenly weren't good enough. They had to be icicle lights, little strands that hang down from the edge of the roof like … well, icicles.

"Here's the next strand," the boy says.

"I need more hooks," I say.

These icicle lights have been around a few years. Last year, you saw them a lot. This year, they are everywhere. Every house and apartment building has them. The restaurants have them. The hair and nail emporiums have them.

Eventually, these icicle lights will be on every home and business in America, one long strand, starting in Maine and zigzagging up and down the country till it reaches the California coast, where someone will wrap it around a sailboat mast in Newport Harbor.

"OK, plug them in," someone in Maine will say, and the whole country will light up at once.

"That'll look nice," says the little girl, when I tell her what's ahead.

"I think you'll like it," I say.

"Can I come up the ladder?" the little girl asks.

"Maybe later," I say.

"OK," she says, sitting back down on the lawn to watch.

The nice thing about a ladder is that I am up here alone, not like on the couch or an easy chair, where I am vulnerable to any kid who passes.

On a ladder, a dad can get a little space. No kids hanging across your shoulders. No one putting pennies down your socks.

"More lights," I tell the boy.

"Huh?"

"Next strand," I tell him.

For the most part, it's an easy installation, a one-story house. There's no tricky second-story work, like my friend J.P. has at his house.

At his house, you have to climb on the roof, then hang over the edge of the second floor, feeling blindly for the edge of the gutter, watching your shadow in the cold, hard driveway below.

That's how J.P. installs lights. He is either the bravest dad I know or a cheap circus act. A suburban acrobat. Cirque du J.P.

"More lights," I tell the boy.

"Huh?"

"Next strand," I tell him.

"Oh," he says, as if this is a surprise that I would ask him for more Christmas lights. For the last 45 minutes, we have been hanging Christmas lights. Each time I ask him for more, he seems surprised. It's a system we've had for several years now.

"Hey, Dad?" he asks.

"What?"

"In the movie 'Scream,' why does she answer the phone the second time?"

"What?"

"When the phone rings the second time, why doesn't Drew Barrymore just let the answering machine get it?" he asks.

It's an interesting question. For some reason, I hadn't considered it much.

"Because she's a Barrymore," I say, hazarding a guess.

"Oh," he says, and goes back to playing his belly like a bongo drum.

"More lights," I tell him.

"Huh?" he says.

* * *

Every December we do this, just as the winds arrive, just as the big gusts flatten Christmas tree lot tents all around Southern California.

Every December these Christmas winds come. They blow extra hard each time some guy climbs a creaky ladder with a string of lights around his neck.

"Careful, Dad," the little girl says when a big gust hits.

"No problem," I say as the ladder wobbles a little.

I grab for the house. The house wobbles a little. I guess that's California for you. Everything's a little wobbly, even the ground.

"Can I come up now?" the little girl asks.

"Not yet," I say.

The kids don't have huge expectations for these new icicle lights. They just hope that they'll turn out to be incredible, that's all, with millions and millions of lights that lure locals and tourists alike to line up for hours in their cars, to drive by our little house and believe in God and Christmas more than ever before. That's all they want from these lights. Nothing more.

"They look OK?" I ask as I hang another set.

"Not really," the little girl says.

Which is when her mother comes outside. Like a lot of mothers, she struggles with Christmas, loves the beauty behind it but is nearly crushed by all the demands – so much so that she is pretty sure that Christmas is a conspiracy to kill her, to sap every last ounce of her strength and leave her sprawled in some mall, with harried shoppers stepping over and around her, hissing at her under their breath.

I assure her that there is no conspiracy. Holidays happen. No one's to blame. At least not in a legal sense.

That's why for Christmas I bought her pearls. Plastic pearls. Ten bucks a box.

"Like the lights, Mom?" the little girl asks, pointing to the house, where I stand like Vanna White, gesturing toward her prize.

My wife looks at the lights. She looks at me on the ladder, wobbling in the winds, grabbing the house for support.

She deserves more than plastic pearls, my wife. She deserves a drink and a winning lottery ticket. She deserves diamonds and a fancy car. Instead, she has us.

"They're beautiful," she says, shielding her eyes from the Christmas winds.

"See, they're beautiful," I tell the boy.

"Huh?" he asks.

"More lights," I say.

December 15, 1999

◆ ◆ ◆

The Football Prenup

THERE is no real explanation for my genial nature and ceaseless, senseless optimism, other than I married well and watch lots of football – primarily the college game, where every fall hope springs eternal.

"Dad, come watch this hook and ladder!" the boy screams as he watches the Nebraska game on TV. "You gotta see this hook-and-ladder play."

"Please don't scream in the house," my wife says calmly.

"Did you see that hook and ladder?" I whisper in her ear, as if reciting a dirty poem.

"Yeah, I saw it," she whispers back.

See? I told you I married well. Like most smart, young brides, she required me to sign a prenuptial football agreement, which prohibits screaming or throwing pillows at the TV – even after interference calls.

It hurt me to sign it, but I loved her more even than I loved Mike Ditka. And I needed a roommate.

So here are the terms of the prenuptial football agreement, signed in blood in the presence of her mother and three humongous hairy people who I think were her uncles – though one of them might have been an aunt:

PRENUPTIAL FOOTBALL AGREEMENT

1. No Astroturf in the house.

2. No eating on the couch.

3. No cursing. Ever.

4. No throwing pillows at the TV.

5. No doing reenactments of favorite plays in football history – such as the Immaculate Reception – in our living room, while wearing only underwear.

6. No screaming "Yeah, baby!" so loud that the cat gets all freaky in the head and starts losing its hair and making devil sounds.

7. No fumble drills during commercials.

8. No barking, spitting or eye gouging. Ever.

9. No comparing the appearance of certain ugly nose guards to her old boyfriends – even if the resemblance is uncanny and legally indisputable.

10. No throwing little rubber footballs across the living room (including screen passes and little safety valves to the backs).

11. Be considerate of fans sitting near you. Behavior that is disruptive to others may result in ejection from the living room.

12. No face-painting the dog.

Now, this is a pretty standard football prenup. Twelve rules, most of them consisting of boilerplate stuff that lawyers keep on their hard drives.

The only items she added were the ones about her old boyfriends and the cat. Like most women, she is unreasonably protective of her cats.

"You're scaring the cat," she said the first time we watched football together in the late '70s.

"It's just a stupid cat," I said.

It was then that I realized it wasn't just a stupid cat. It was like a reincarnation of every close friend she'd ever had, every soul mate, every good listener with which she shared intimate secrets late in the night. That's how women see cats. As keepers of their souls.

She was so mad about the cat that when I asked her to sit on my lap and feed me Doritos, she refused, even though when we first met she said she'd be glad to sit on my lap and feed me Doritos for the rest of our lives, freeing up my hands to do whirlybird gestures at the TV and throw pillows at the refs.

Then I mentioned the cat, and the next thing I know, she's making me sign this football prenup and we're having a few kids. As you've probably noticed, life happens pretty fast. All of which brings us to today.

Oklahoma 24, Nebraska 14, second half just underway.

"Yeah, baby!" screams the boy as Oklahoma scores again.

"Yeah, baby!" screams the little girl.

"Oh, my God," my wife mutters, throwing her arms in the air, inadvertently signaling a touchdown.

* * *

In the late afternoon, we go out to the empty high school field to practice extra points and field goals and throw the ball around a little, like families do on fall days when the trees are blushing.

"Here, let me kick," says the little girl.

"Me first," says her brother, who's been kicking extra points for years now.

So the little girl watches her brother nail extra points, watches him cream kick after kick through the uprights. First from 15 yards, then 20. Even 30.

Then the little girl tries, from the one-yard line, with a little blue UCLA football that's apparently made of Flubber, because somehow it actually goes through the uprights on her first attempt.

"Touchdown!" she screams, convinced that this game is easy.

"Yeah, baby!" screams her brother.

Eventually, my goal is to get the whole family kicking extra points – even my lovely and patient older daughter, who doesn't have much time for football these days, what with studying calculus till she's cross-eyed and filling out college applications.

I try to explain to her that kicking extra points might be a nice thing to list on her college applications, under extracurricular activities.

"Kicked extra points with my dad," she'd write, which would be spotted by some sharp-eyed admissions officer at Brown or Dartmouth, where they are always looking for students with the right stuff, not to mention reliable place-kickers.

"Extra points?" my lovely and patient daughter asks.

"Yeah, we're all kicking them," I explain. "Even Mom."

"I'll pass," she says.

"We do that too," I say.

"Maybe next time," my daughter says, looking at me cross-eyed, like I'm some sort of calculus problem. Which I probably am.

"We'll save a spot for you on the team," I promise her.

"Thanks," she says.

November 8, 2000

♦ ♦ ♦

Savoring Summer

WE'RE going for a walk on a summer's night, the little cocker spaniel pulling and pulling along the still-warm suburban pavement. His own Iditarod. Baked Alaska.

"Mush," I say, as he pulls me down one street, then up another.

"You're an animal," I tell him, exaggerating only a little.

And he pulls and pulls till I snap the leash, which is his signal to quit pulling and lick the barbecue sauce off my ankle. I never taught him to lick the barbecue sauce off my ankle. Somehow, he just knows.

"Listen," I say, and he stops to listen to the freeway half a mile away.

It's our ocean, this freeway. At least that's what a real estate agent once told us. "Sounds like the ocean," she said – the soft whoosh of cars, the rumble of trucks.

"Tide's coming in," I tell the dog, and he believes me, then licks my ankle again.

"Mush," I say.

Each night, we take this walk. Each night he pulls and pulls, and I hold on tight, walking a mile, maybe two. Sometimes I bring a beer in case one of us overheats.

"I'm hot," he always says, mostly with his eyes.

"Just keep walking," I tell him.

I can't imagine summer without a dog, without taking these lazy walks on long June evenings when the sun takes two hours to set, always lingering, the sky sort of buttery.

"Slow down," I tell him, because little dogs are like little men, bursting with energy, always in a rush.

"Just slow down," I say, savoring summer.

Not once have we ever gotten lost. We wander out across this maze of sub-urban streets and houses that all look alike, and not once have we ever gotten lost. Confused, maybe. Disoriented, always. But never lost.

"Where are we going next?" I ask him.

And he pulls me around the corner.

"I'm hot," he says again, looking at my beer.

"Just keep walking," I tell him.

As we head up the next street, I tell him about some of the great places I've walked. Chicago. New Orleans. Des Moines.

"Pasadena's nice," I tell him. "You'd like Pasadena."

I tell him about all the great shade trees in Pasadena. And all the fire hydrants. The bushes.

"Pasadena might be the dog-walking capital of America," I tell him, exaggerating only a little.

And finally, we head for home, lured back by the sound of a kitchen blender playing softly in the distance, played by someone who knows what he's doing. Blend. Puree. Liquefy. Songs for a summer's night.

"If we're lucky, they'll make us something," I say as we turn in the driveway.

"Mush," I tell him one last time.

Sometimes the people who live here greet us on the porch, coughing their summer coughs, welcoming us home like the cast of Cirque du Soleil, tumbling and sailing through the air, crawling over one another, then stepping on my hand.

"Thanks," I say as I sit on the porch steps.

"What for, Dad?" they ask.

"For stepping on my hand," I say.

"Sorry," they all say, not sure exactly which one of them stepped on my hand. Might've been all three.

And they stand around for a while, sniffing the warm night air, watching the stars, listening to the freeway.

"Tide's coming in," the boy says, and the dog licks his ankle.

They are summer kids, their skin still holding in the day's heat, like the pavement we just walked on.

They live mostly in towels, spending their afternoons squeezing pool water from their hair and dripping Popsicles onto their stomachs.

At night, they mostly drip watermelon, and those icy drinks they make in the blender.

One of the kids is still wearing sunglasses – the short one, which is the one you always need to beware of.

"I can feel his heart," she says, crawling over my back.

"Where?" the others ask, talking as if I'm not even around.

"Right here," says the little red-haired girl, her hand approximately where my kidneys should be.

"That's his wallet," the boy says.

"No, that's his heart," the little girl says.

The rest of the evening continues pretty much like this. Somebody spills her strawberry smoothie in my hair. Someone else lifts my wallet. Someone steps on my hand again.

"Thanks," I say.

"Sorry," they all say.

In the distance, a police car sings.

"What's going on out here?" their mother asks as she joins us on the porch.

"Mostly, I'm being mugged," I say.

"I have his wallet," the boy says.

"Here, feel his heart," the little girl says.

"Want to go for a walk?" their mother asks.

"Thought you'd never ask," I say.

And back down the driveway we go.

June 30, 1999

◆ ◆ ◆

Still My Valentine

I am considered "a catch" only in certain Third World countries, where my limited ability to read and write and my fondness for simple things like the squeeze bunt and a good crisp apple are not viewed as a lack of sophistication, as they often are here in America, in our First World home.

So Valentine's Day takes on added significance for me. Each year, I must woo my wife again, start from scratch really. In marriage, there's no such thing as tenure.

"Too bad there isn't tenure," I told her once.

"What are you talking about?" she asked.

"In marriage," I said. "After 10 years, you should get tenure."

It was then that she explained to me there never would be tenure. Not in our marriage.

I was to treat her as if sometime in the night, a spell washed over her and she forgot who I was. In the morning, we would wake up and begin our courtship from scratch. Roses. Edible underwear. The whole thing. For about two days, I found this hugely arousing.

"Can't do it," I told my wife on the third day.

"What's that?"

"Woo you every day," I told her.

Wooing is a lot of work. Especially at my age. To woo a woman all over again takes a certain creative flair that I don't possess. Or a strong chin, which I don't have either. A wallet the size of a Buick surely doesn't hurt. I don't even have a Buick the size of a Buick. Mostly, I stick with sensible foreign cars.

"What are you doing for Valentine's Day?" I ask my friend Paul.

"What'd you have in mind?" he answers.

See what a funny guy he is? He gets most of his jokes from his retiree father, who e-mails them to him from Texas. If it weren't for his father, Paul wouldn't be funny at all.

"For Sara," I ask. "What are you getting her?"

Paul is in the same boat I am. We've both been married since the Polk administration. Our wives are both lovely and smart and wise to our ways. In short, they're on to us.

"Valentine's Day? Beats me," Paul says, then tells me a joke about a guy who wandered into a bar with an alligator.

So I am on my own this Valentine's. I head for the drugstore, looking for love. I find it in Aisle 8, near the umbrellas and bottled bleach.

"Even after all this time and all we've been through, I still have trouble finding ways to show my love for you," the greeting card says.

Like you, I am constantly amazed at how expensive love can be. Loneliness, in the long run, costs more. But love is no bargain. These greeting cards run $4.95 a pop; $6.49 in Canada.

"But the plain and simple truth is, I'm an ordinary guy who's happy you still love me – though I sometimes wonder why," the card says.

What mush. So I call my friend Jeff, a ticket broker who can get me in almost anywhere. According to him, a good date will do wonders for a relationship. He should know. The guy has a beautiful wife and four lovely daughters. And he's not even as good-looking as me.

"What about Romeo and Juliet?" I ask him.

"Dead," he says. "Both of them."

"Actually, I was asking about tickets," I say.

It could be a perfect Valentine's gift. A night out to see the stage production of "Romeo and Juliet." Romantic. Elegant. Timeless.

I can see us in the Ahmanson Theatre. My wife would sit there admiring the language and the beautiful set while I would snore softly in the seat next to her, yelling at Kobe Bryant from time to time in my sleep.

"PASS THE BALL!" I would scream aloud, like I often do in my sleep. "PASS THE STINKIN' BALL!"

Properly timed, it would add a dimension to Shakespeare that even he couldn't have imagined.

"A hundred," my friend Jeff says.

"Apiece?" I ask.

"Yep," he says. "Valentine's night is a little more expensive."

Can't do it. Paid 200 bucks last weekend for new tires, tapping into our emergency fund and our main budget. This was a real emergency. The steel belts were showing through.

"What are you doing for Valentine's?" I ask the boy.

I'm so desperate now, I am asking a kid who once sprinkled Sweet Tarts on his salad.

The boy considers the question seriously for a moment, then sneezes and falls down, blown over by his own sneeze.

"Valentine's Day?" he asks from the living room floor. "I thought that was in April."

I move on.

"What are you doing for Valentine's?" I ask the little girl, who knows a thing or two about love.

Twice now, she has been invited to boy-girl birthday parties.

"We're only having a party for 20 minutes," she complains, explaining her school's plans for Valentine's.

"Last year, we got an hour," she says. "And we got to watch 'Winnie-the-Pooh.' "

"Romance is dead," I tell her.

"Huh?"

"Never mind," I say.

Which brings us to this morning, Valentine's morning, with everything awash in red, the color of love and war, and me with no plans for dinner and still no gift.

So I will feed my wife chocolates and rub her tummy, like I used to when she was pregnant and full of dreams for us.

I will feed her chocolates and woo her and make her laugh, the way I used to when we had no money and it was all I could give her. Which is pretty much the way things are now, what with the new tires and all.

"Did you hear the one about the guy who wandered into a bar with an alligator?" I'll ask her.

"No," she'll say, hoping that somewhere amid all the jokes, there'll be some little hint of how much I love her.

There is. Happy Valentine's, honey.

February 14, 2001

The More, the Merrier

WE are fortunate with friends. Bad with money. Lousy with real estate. But rich with friends. Crazy friends. Funny friends. Generous friends. Frankly, I'd prefer the money, though nobody ever really asked.

"We're going to the mountains," my wife explains.

"With friends?" I ask.

"Of course," she says.

So we head up into the mountains for spring vacation with the Beverly Hills dentist and her funny husband and their three children, a convoy of kids and ski clothes and fishing gear, luggage and shoes stuffed in every available corner of our cars.

Close the minivan door and shoelaces dangle out, dancing in the wind.

"Dad, my laces are stuck in the door," the boy says as we pull away.

"So are mine," I say.

Up the steep roads we go, behind Pepsi truck drivers who never look back, through the haze and the clouds, till we reach our Shangri-La, a little mountain town with an IHOP on the corner.

"This is it?" asks my lovely and patient older daughter.

"Nice, huh?" I say.

"This is it?" she asks again.

There was a time, not that long ago, when spring vacation meant stuffing two T-shirts in a bag and heading to Florida or Texas with a bunch of college buddies. If there was room, you took a toothbrush.

Once there, you'd meet smiley girls from Ohio or Missouri in cutoff jeans and bikini tops. If you were lucky, they would ask you to apply their suntan lotion. Buy them a beer. Swim in the sea at midnight, naked as a porpoise.

After four days, they would leave for home. Then more girls would arrive in jeans and bikini tops. Thirsty girls with winter skin, cooking quickly in the April sun.

"Can you help me with this Coppertone?" they'd purr.

Fortunately, those days are long gone.

"Dad-Dad-Dad-Dad-Dad," says a voice from the back seat, nearly waking me.

"What?"

"My stomach really hurts," the voice says.

"We're almost there," I say.

"I think I'm gonna hurl," the voice says.

"Let me out!" her brother yells. "Let me out!"

At the rental house, we unpack the cars. Because we all work together, it only takes a day.

On Sunday, we ski.

They are soft, these slopes, the mountain turning into a giant Slurpee in the spring heat. Icy but drinkable. In the million-ounce size.

"This is great," says the boy.

"It's a little slushy," the boy's buddy says.

As with most family vacations, it becomes an Iron Dad competition. One day we ski. The next, we ride horses. One morning, we go bowling. Yes, bowling. For 45 minutes, it is the most fun the kids have ever had. Then they sober up.

"Can we go fishing?" the little girl asks.

"Absolutely," I say.

"I mean today," she says.

"Oh," I say.

The little red-haired girl is rich with friends as well. They join us fishing, three little girls in all, with their Little Mermaid fishing rods and a Styrofoam container of worms. Medium night crawlers. Twenty to a container.

"We're ready," the little girls say, wearing sunglasses and $60 shoes, looking like a Nordstrom ad.

And we find a mountain lake that sparkles, fed by snowmelt and stocked with trout by the fine state of California, which knows a thing or two about stocking lakes.

"Watch the holes," I tell the girls as we walk from the parking lot.

"What holes?" they ask.

Along the path, there are these holes. Dug by ground squirrels, probably. The holes are the size of billiard pockets, just big enough for a kid. One false step and the little girls would be gone, fishing poles and all.

Whoosh, and one would disappear. Whoosh, there'd go another.

"Where are the girls?" the mothers would ask when I got home. And I'd be forced to go back to find them.

"Watch the holes," I warn the girls as we walk.

Finally, we reach the water's edge. I open the tackle box. It has hooks five sizes too large. A jar of salmon eggs older than God. A tiny tube of Mary Kay sunscreen.

The little girls dig in the container for worms. When they are done, they wipe their hands on my sleeve.

"Thanks," I say.

"Sure, Dad," says the little girl.

To our right, the sun is sinking fast, leaving the lake sparkling white, like tonic water.

In the distance, the ski slopes are turning purple, then gold.

"We're in luck," I say.

"Why, Dad?"

"Because we're here," I tell the girls.

"Why, Dad?" the little girl asks, still puzzled.

"We just are," I say.

April 12, 2000

◆ ◆ ◆

So Long, Charlie Brown

YOU have hair like Terry Bradshaw and a head shaped like a football helmet.

Your kite doesn't fly. The baseball team seldom wins. The Valentine never arrives. For 50 years, you've worn the same shirt. But you never blame others for your problems.

You're a good man, Charlie Brown.

"Well, we're all set for the picnic," a Peanuts character says.

"Here's the ice cream," says a second kid, opening a container of ice cream.

"And here's the cake," another kid says, opening a cake box.

Off to the side stands Charlie Brown, cupping something in his hands.

"What are you holding in your hands, Charlie Brown?"

"Soup," he says.

When Charles Schulz was in kindergarten, a teacher spotted a sketch he'd done and told him that someday he'd be an artist.

In high school, he took an art-school correspondence course. Cost his dad, a barber, 170 bucks.

Schulz's first job was doing the lettering on comics drawn by other people. One day, he drew a cartoon of a young boy sitting on a curb and holding a baseball bat.

"Sparky, I think you should draw more of those little kids," another illustrator advised him. "They're pretty good."

"It's a high fly ball," several Peanuts characters yell.

"Catch it, Charlie Brown!"

"Catch it, and the championship is ours!"

"Have you got it, Charlie Brown?"

"Don't miss it!"

"Get under it, Charlie Brown!"

"Isn't this exciting?"

"What if he drops it?"

"If he drops it, let's all kick him."

Schulz had five children of his own. They eventually grew up. But the Peanuts characters never did. They were stuck in the third grade forever.

Smart. Cruel. Sensitive. Sweet. They faked their way through book reports.

Lied about missing homework. Forgot their lines in school plays. All skills they could use later in life. For third-graders, they acted a lot like adults.

"Oh, I won't pull the ball away, Charlie Brown," Lucy says. "I give you my bonded word."

"All right, I'll trust you," Charlie Brown says. "I have an underlying faith in human nature. I believe that people who want to change can do so. And I believe that they should be given the chance to prove themselves."

At the last second, of course, Lucy pulls the ball away, leaving Charlie flat on his back.

"Aaugh!" he says.

"Charlie Brown, your faith in human nature is an inspiration to all young people," Lucy says.

This is how good Schulz's work is. It holds up in mere words. No drawings required.

One moment, he'll be quoting Rudyard Kipling. Another, he's making fun of pop psychology.

He also had a way of fast-forwarding a conversation, the way a witty novelist or screenwriter might, skipping the obvious response and jumping to something else unexpectedly.

Most of all, he found humor in the tiny, vulnerable moments we all experience. His comic strips had more humanity than most of today's movies.

And he did it mostly with his words.

"Tonight is Halloween," Lucy tells Linus. "How come you're not sitting out in a pumpkin patch waiting for the Great Pumpkin and making a total, complete and absolute fool of yourself?"

"You have a nice way of wording things," Linus says.

"Thank you," Lucy says. "I work them out on little slips of paper beforehand."

It is, at least in my mind, one of the longest creative bursts in American history. More than 18,000 comic strips, running daily for almost 50 years.

Like most Americans, I don't remember a time when there wasn't Peanuts. I don't remember a time when Charles Schulz wasn't at the top of the page.

And on Sunday, this grand run ends. Due to his much-publicized illness, Schulz's last original comic strip appears this weekend, at the top of the comics page, where it has been forever.

"The bases are loaded again, and there's still nobody out," Schroeder tells Charlie Brown one spring day on the pitcher's mound.

"So what do you think?" Charlie Brown finally asks.

"We live in difficult times," Schroeder says.

So long, slugger.

February 9, 2000

So This Is Fatherhood

THE tomatoes are doing well so far, the ones we planted in big pots by the front porch. "Better Boys." "Early Girls." And that new hybrid, the Bette Midlers.

"What next, Dad? Soybeans?" my lovely and patient older daughter asks.

"Cocktail onions," I tell her.

She ignores me, as always, and goes back to planting her flowers.

That's right, a teenager is helping her parents plant flowers. Just when you think there are things you can count on, just when you think your teenagers will not lift a finger to help out around the house and the world is a cold, cruel place with no real future, along comes a kid with trays of petunias and geraniums to plant in the front flower bed. On a nice June Sunday, no less.

"You think you know people," I tell her mother as our teenager unloads another tray of flowers.

"What, Dad?" my daughter asks.

"Over there," I say, pointing her toward the flower bed.

We communicate mostly by sign language now, my teenage daughter and me. She is 17. I am 177. I speak, increasingly, in this Walter Matthau mumble that the late actor willed to me when he left this earth back in July. Thank you, God. I got Matthau's mumble.

"No, not there," I say.

"Huh?" says my daughter.

"Over there," I mumble.

"Huh?"

I point the shovel to where I want the flowers. She says, "Why didn't you just say so?" I say, "I did." She says, "Huh?" And we go on about our work.

It is not until we are in our 40s, really, that we understand our fathers.

Oh, sure, we think we understand them in our 20s when our own kids are born and we get up in the morning to oatmeal-splattered walls and sofas that smell like last week's diapers.

We think we understand our fathers in our 30s when we struggle to make the mortgage and try to straighten out our Fred Flintstone golf swings.

But it isn't until our 40s that we truly start to understand them. Our fathers' long trek. Parenthood's million-mile journey.

"Dad!"

"Huh?"

"A spider!" the little girl says.

The little girl is helping her sister with the flowers the way I help with Thanksgiving dinner – that is, mostly by standing around and commenting and getting in the way.

The little girl has seen so many Olsen twins movies that she has ceased to be a contributing member of society. Usually, she just stands around like one of the Olsen twins and comments on things she knows nothing about, then waits for the studio audience to respond. Which it never does.

"That's not a spider," I say.

"It's not?"

"That's a butterfly," I say.

"No, Dad, that's a spider," my older daughter says.

"If you leave it alone, it'll grow into a butterfly," I say.

"No, you mean caterpillars," the little girl says. "Caterpillars turn into butterflies."

"They do?" I say.

"Yep."

"OK, then it's a caterpillar," I say.

"Dad, it's a spider!" my older daughter huffs.

After many years, I'm starting to think my daughters have really bad eyesight. They seem to see things for what they are.

As a modern American father, I don't see things for what they are. I see things the way they should be, and ask why not. It's a Kennedy thing. Robert Kennedy, I think. Or maybe George.

"Look, Dad, a palindrome," my older daughter says proudly when she gets the flowers lined up.

"What's a palindrome?" the little girl asks.

"A palindrome is something that looks the same forwards and backwards," my older daughter explains.

"See? Red, blue, red, blue, red," my older daughter says, pointing at the order she's planted the flowers. "A palindrome."

I'd always thought a palindrome had to be a word or a phrase.

A man, a plan, a canal, Panama.

Read it forward, read it backward. It reads the same. A palindrome.

"A palindrome can be anything," my older daughter tells me.

"It can be a flower bed?" I ask.

"Sure."

"It can be vomit?" her little sister asks.

"Don't be disgusting," I tell the little girl.

"I'm just a kid, Dad," she explains.

"Well, it's starting to show," I say.

Our fathers gave the world television; we gave the world personal computers.

Our fathers had John Wayne; we have Sylvester Stallone.

Our fathers never touched a dish or a diaper; we sometimes behave like Hazel.

My own dad used to grow rows of green beans and tomatoes, planted like

Marine platoons, in perfect lines; me, I have palindromes.

For the fathers of the world, some things have gotten better. Some things have gotten worse.

I miss my dad. Left seven years ago to save Walter Matthau a spot on the couch.

I'll bet they're having a good time up there, raising tomatoes and mumbling to each other about the things they like. The Cubs. Cocktail onions. Ann-Margret.

"Look, Dad, a moth," says the little girl.

"That's not a moth," I say.

"It's not?"

"That's a hummingbird," I say.

Happy Father's Day.

June 13, 2001

◆ ◆ ◆

Dodger Blues

TONIGHT it's just us and 26,000 other Dodger assistant coaches, heading out to Chavez Ravine for dinner or a light snack. A little after 7, the floor show begins.

"Who's on the hill?" I ask.

"Hershiser," says the boy.

"Good," I say.

We get our program, then head for our seats on this warm Monday evening, up the escalator and through the turnstiles, excited by the sight of the Dodger field. It never fails, this low-grade buzz I get from a whiff of ballpark grass.

"Look at Brito," I tell the boy.

"Where?"

"Right there," I say.

Who can miss Dodger scout Mike Brito, in a suit the color of a dollar bill, standing behind the backstop in his trademark hat?

Dodger ushers have done away with their hats, but not Brito. He looks like a Kentucky horse trainer. Or the mayor in a Meredith Willson musical.

He stands at the backstop with his radar gun and pitching book. Every once in a while, someone stops by for a picture. Like a good politician, he obliges.

"Look at Brito," the boy says, as he poses with a pretty fan.

"He's like the mayor," I say.

"Really?" the boy asks.

"Mayor Brito," I say

* * *

And look at us, finally making it out to Dodger Stadium for only the second time this season. A slow start. Embarrassing, really. Only two games by late June. Somewhere along the line, our priorities got all messed up.

"Who's pitching?" my wife asks.

"Hershiser," the boy says again.

"Is he good?" the little girl asks.

"Very good," I say.

Not tonight. In the second frame, things fall quickly apart. There's a walk. Then a home run. A couple more walks. A single. A wild pitch. A hit batter. Another walk.

By the time the second inning is over, Orel Hershiser, Dodger icon, has given up eight runs. You could almost cry for the guy.

"Look at him," I tell my wife as he walks from the field with his head down, like a guy suffering from cluster headaches.

"Poor Orel," says my wife.

Then a remarkable thing happens. The Dodger fans begin to applaud. As Hershiser heads to the dugout, the fans rise out of their seats – something Dodger fans are not prone to do – and give him an ovation. Not for tonight. For all those other nights, when everyone was younger and the right arm had some snap to it and the Dodgers traveled the country like the young gods of baseball. For that, they applaud.

"That's pretty classy," I tell the boy.

"What?"

"The way they're applauding him," I say. "That's pretty classy."

"Sure, Dad," he says.

Down 8-1 in the third inning, we eat a little, then sit back and enjoy the sideshows.

* * *

There are always good sideshows at Dodger games. Funny hats. Beach balls. Unmercifully large tattoos. Young women with older men. Married couples. Unmarried couples. Vendors with pinkeye. Young toughs on dates. Church groups.

One big, rollicking Dodger family, soaking up a summer evening.

Out on the field, things are pretty relaxed as well. The Dodgers are playing defense like they don't want to get their uniforms dirty, like they have to go home after the game and wash them themselves.

The guy sitting next to me has more dirt on him. I guess he plays to win.

"How'd you get so dirty?" I ask the boy.

"I fell," he says.

"Where?"

"In my nacho dish," he says, wiping cheese from his nose and elbow.

He's a gamer, this kid. An eater and a gamer.

So I tell him about some of the great food-related feats I have seen a Dodger Stadium.

I tell them all about how my friend Irving once set a Dodger Stadium record by eating two Dodger Dogs in the course of one Raul Mondesi strikeout.

Four pitches, two hot dogs. The second was a slider. Not the hot dog, the pitch. About 85 mph, it gave Irving time to swallow the first Dodger Dog and pick up the second one.

"To this day, it's the most amazing athletic feat I've ever seen," I tell the kids.

"Wow," says the little girl.

"Did he burp?" the boy asks.

"All through the next inning," I say.

"Wow," says the little girl.

"And when he did, three people in front of us died," I say.

"Really?" asks the little girl.

"Wow," says the boy.

Out on the field, another Dodger hitter strikes out, taking a wild whack at what would've been ball four. A good walk spoiled.

"You think we're going to win?" asks the little girl.

"Sure," I say.

By the eighth inning, the floor show is almost over. Of 26,000 people who showed up to watch the slumping Dodgers, only a few are left.

* * *

We sit in our seats, listening to a Billy Joel song being played on the stadium organ – just us and Brito and a few thousand others. There's no quit in Brito. You have to admire that.

"Look, there's Vin Scully," I tell the little girl, pointing to the press box.

"Is he the announcer?" she asks.

"I think so," I say.

"He's doing a good job," she says.

In the ninth, the Dodgers load the bases. Shawn Gilbert, a sturdy young man batting .063, comes to the plate.

He lofts a 2-1 pitch into the evening air, a loopy little hit that lands like a sparrow between the center fielder and his neighbor. Two runs score. The night, once again, is alive.

"I think we're going to win," says the little girl, as the Dodgers pull within striking distance.

"No more beer for you," I say.

"I don't drink beer," she says.

"Thank goodness for that," I say.

And with that, the last Dodger lines out.

June 28, 2000

◆ ◆ ◆

Funny Thing, a Christmas Tree

WE drive, the dog and I, down the boulevard and across Los Angeles, a livable little town with plenty going for it: mini-malls and car dealerships, store-front psychics and dozens of Christmas tree lots.

"We flock," the sign at the Christmas tree lot says. "White. Pink. Blue. Glitter."

Welcome to L.A. Welcome to our Christmas.

"I think I'll get you flocked," I tell the dog. "For Christmas, I mean."

And he looks at me the way I look at a plate of the finest lamb chops, drooling a little, tinsel in his eyes. It's hard to describe the way he looks at me. It's hard to describe real love.

"Quit staring," I finally have to tell him.

Down the boulevard we go. The dog loves riding in the car like this, returning the Blockbuster videos or off to buy milk. Occasionally, the hardware store.

These are big events in his life, as in mine. We head off early. A full tank of gas.

"OK, where next?" I ask.

He just shrugs. He doesn't care. He's happy everywhere we go. Dog happy. As happy as anything can get.

"Surprise me," he says.

So I do. We spin by the ATM, then to the dry cleaners.

For lunch, I buy him a doughnut – glazed, his favorite – which he eats in one breath. I don't blame him. Basically, he eats like I do. One bite per meal.

"Wanna buy some lottery tickets?" I ask.

It's maybe the dumbest question he's ever heard. He'd love to buy lottery tickets. Down the boulevard we go.

We are entering middle age together, the dog and I. In a few more years, our ears will be equally hairy. Then our prostates will go. We'll while away the afternoons baking bread and watching game shows.

"This is great," I'll tell him.

"Let's go for a ride," he'll say.

With that to look forward to, we run our errands.

As I drive, he watches me work the car. He sits in the passenger seat, winking at me with one eye, then the other. Like most dogs, he has two brains, one to operate each eye. When he winks at me, I wink back.

"Nice turn," he winks as I pull into the post office.

"Thanks," I say.

"Nice stop," he winks as I pull into a parking space.

"Thanks," I say.

Mostly, I think he wishes I'd stop at one of these Christmas tree lots. He loves Christmas tree lots. To a dog, there can never be enough trees. Especially in L.A. He thinks they put these extra trees out just for him.

"They're not for you," I tell him.

"They're not?"

"No, they're for everyone," I tell him.

So we drive past the Christmas tree lots, him kissing the windows clean, me licking my Coke.

As we pass the trees, I think about my friend Bill, who is taking his family on a train ride this weekend to get their Christmas tree. First, you get on a train, then they take you to the trees. You cut your tree, then put it on the train.

It's one of those elaborate things only great family men like Bill will do. He'll call, make the reservation, then spend his Sunday on a Christmas tree train.

Of all the people with Christmas tree war stories, Bill may have the best ones. There was the time the tree fell off the car. Or the time they couldn't get the tree out of the station wagon. Apparently, the branches had grown on the way home, and they couldn't get it out.

Then there was the time he went to lop an inch off the bottom with his nice chain saw, and hit some big spike the Christmas tree guys left in there. He's a lawyer, though, so they gave him a new chain. And a down payment on a house.

"I wonder ... ," I say to myself as the dog and I drive down the boulevard.

And what I'm wondering is this: As Bill gets off the train to get a Christmas tree 50 miles away, what if I go over to his yard and cut one down? He's got a few nice noble firs in the corner of the yard. He might not even miss it. Just in case, I'd leave a note.

"Dear Bill," the note would say. "Thank you for the tree. My wife just had to have it. You had many, so I didn't think you'd mind."

I'd sign it "your grateful neighbor," nothing more, then leave it by the door.

Generally, I'm not much for pranks. Most of the time, they can be mean-spirited and boorish. But it's Christmas.

Here's another one I've always wanted to try.

I'd wait till my friend Don bought a tree, because I know my friend Don and I know he'd get a great big tree and keep it in the garage till they put it up.

Then each night, I'd sneak into his garage and replace it with a tree just a few inches smaller. One day, his lovely wife would notice.

"It's shrinking," his lovely wife would say.

"Christmas trees can't shrink," her lovely husband would answer.

Finally, when it was down to 2 feet tall, I'd have it flocked. Pink. Blue. Maybe glitter.

"Dear Don," the note would read. "Merry Christmas."

December 6, 2000

CHAPTER SEVEN

THE BABY

◆ ◆ ◆

Another Kid? At Your Age?

No one ever claimed biology was particularly pretty, especially when your mom and dad are involved.

"I'm going to have a baby," their mother announces.

One kid cries. Another nearly passes out from shock and disgust. Generally, everyone takes it quite well.

"Hey, Mom," the boy asks every morning, "how do you like your eggs?"

"Unfertilized," she grumbles, a joke the kids repeat to everyone who walks in the door. Believe me, walk in the door, you'll hear that joke.

"Hey, Dad, how does Mom like her eggs?"

"Over easy?"

"Unfertilized!" they scold.

"I'll try to remember that," I say.

Yes, the issue of contraception has come up, and you know your life has turned upside-down when your teenage kids are slipping you hints about such things and chastising you for your lack of self-control.

With unusual glee, our lovely and patient older daughter lectures us about what an unplanned pregnancy can do to someone's life. Evidently, having a child is a huge, lifelong responsibility.

"Are you sure you're ready for this?" our college-age daughter asks.

"Somehow, we'll make it work," I assure her.

"We're young," her mother notes, "but we love each other."

"Well, sometimes that's not enough," our daughter says.

And sometimes it is. It got us through our first three children, who are turning out pretty well despite a chronic shortage of funds and a surplus of those parenting books their mother keeps buying. Somehow, they survived all that. Now they'll probably survive this.

"Grandma, can I come live with you?" the older daughter pleads over the phone.

"Me, too!" yells the little girl.

First, they were forced to endure the house renovation, which has lasted longer than the Civil War and shows no sign of ever ending.

Now there's this new baby on the way. Talk about war. Talk about sacrifice. Clothes. Food. Proms. Tuition. The kids can somehow sense the new set of demands that will be placed upon the family.

"I'm not changing any diapers," the boy says.

"Me either," says his little sister.

"Me either," I lie.

Of course, the biological details of it all continue to baffle them. Just how does something like this happen to parents in their 40s?

At 40, the number of eggs drops. They are good eggs, mostly, just fewer of them. This, according to experts and dads everywhere, reduces the chances of conception.

Among married couples, it can also lead to a certain recklessness. It can lead to surprise. How do you like your eggs? Well, you know.

Then there is the rarity of husband-wife romance itself, what with kids sleeping with the parents, as many children do these days.

You know how it goes. During a house renovation, you lose a bedroom, some kid is in bed with you. Even when you're not renovating, someone is having a nightmare and tiptoeing around the bedroom like a cat burglar.

"Mom?"

"Huh?

"Nightmare," someone says, which can put a crimp in the marital relations department, if you know what I mean.

So how does something like this happen?

"Did you go on a cruise?" our friend Mary Ann asks. "Usually, it happens on a cruise."

No, not a cruise. Rarely left the house, though in hindsight that was probably a mistake. In my experience, most accidents happen in the home.

"I'm going with an Immaculate Conception," I explain to my friend Paul.

"That's what you said last time," Paul says.

I favor the Immaculate Conception explanation, since it hints that God is somehow involved and it would free me of original sin. Any time you can unload sin, original or not, sign me up.

"Actually, I think it was the night of Taylor's slumber party," my wife explains.

"So if Taylor doesn't have a slumber party, none of this happens?" I ask.

"That's right, slugger," she says.

Can life be more capricious? Can the turning points be more unpredictable?

Can humor, faith, persistence, wisdom and family see you through? Not likely. But what else are you going to do?

"It's a boy," predicts my buddy Irv.

"It is?" I say.

"If I'm wrong, it'll be the first time."

If you ask him, Irv will also predict the due date and describe what you had for dinner the night the baby was conceived. It's a gift, possibly. Or a form of dementia.

"I'm never wrong," he says. "Just ask Metzker."

Like I have the time. Ask my buddy Metzker something, and you'd better carve out a week. Love the guy. But he requires a lot of patience.

"Just ask him," says Irv.

OK, someday I'll ask him. In the meantime, I'll sit here wondering how I'll pay for these new additions to the family – the house and the kid.

Of course, I've been wondering about such things for nearly 20 years now. There are finger-sized channels in my forehead from all the rubbing and worrying, worrying and rubbing. It's one of the components of aging, I suppose. But things usually work out. Somehow we manage.

"Hey, Mom, how do you like your eggs?" someone asks her yet again.

"Grown and out of the house," she teases.

Not for a while.

July 31, 2002

◆ ◆ ◆

Sure Signs of a New Season

IN this week's diary of a mad suburb, we find that autumn has arrived, the children have gone back to school and a pregnant woman is chasing ants around her new kitchen, the one with the brushed stainless-steel appliances and the new chrome toaster, all sullied by these ants. Ants. Ants. Everywhere ants.

"It's like I have to get up 10 minutes early just to start killing them," my wife notes.

"And we appreciate that," I say.

In the last few weeks, she's become like a character out of "The Sopranos," pregnant and homicidal at the same time, killing things just as she is giving life to others. It's one of those contradictions you find a lot in an American suburb.

"I think," she tells me, "you're going to have to crawl under the house and spray."

Sure, I could do that. But this is her war. Fights it like this every fall. And if she's not slaying ants, who knows where her attention may turn.

"Don't bring me into this," I say.

"Look, look!" she says.

"Huh?"

"They're coming from under the stove," she says.

As Cheever and Updike found, a suburb is no place for a grown man. A suburb is a great place for a kid or a mom or a nice tomato garden. But not necessarily for a man.

Men need more activities. They need a trout pond in the mountains, or a ballpark on a city street. A suburb has neither of these. All a suburb has is, well ...

"Ants," I say to my friend Bill. "You guys have ants?"

"Sure," he says, "everyone has ants this time of year."

"So what do you do about them?"

"We just learn to love 'em," he says.

Fat chance. Not in the suburbs. Generally, a suburb is not a place renowned for its tolerance.

I suspect Bill is climbing under the house right now with a flashlight and a can of Raid and wondering if he's being watched by creatures that can see in the dark. Skunks. Black widows. The widows' attorneys. Sweating a little, all of them.

That's what Bill is doing. Firing his big, blue can of unscented Raid in the dark at ant trails, real and imagined, then high-tailing it back to the warm glow of a football game on TV. I know Bill too well. I know his wife, too.

Back at our house, meanwhile, the Sopranos are taking a stab at tolerance.

"You know what Bill says?" I ask my wife.

"I can't wait," she says.

"Bill says they like their ants," I tell her. "Can't get enough."

"Really?"

"That's what he said."

"Then you can take him our ants," she says.

"Who?" I say.

"Bill," she says.

"What about him?" I ask.

To this day, I have poor communication skills, a shortcoming I blame on a childhood of listening to Chicago politicians mangle the language, then get reelected anyway, time and again. One hand on the microphone, another doing deals behind your back.

Daley. Roman Pucinski. Even Abe Gibron. What kind of role models were these for Chicago's schoolkids? You'd sit in class learning about syntax, then go home and listen to a bunch of marble-mouthed public figures substituting "da" for "the" and "dere-fore" for "therefore" on the evening news.

After a childhood of that, it's no wonder my marriage has moments of absolute unclarity. It's amazing I can speak at all.

"Oooooo," my wife says.

"What now?"

"The baby just kicked," she says.

My wife stands there rubbing her tummy, big as a bowling ball and active, too. She is now seven months along with this miracle pregnancy, proof that no matter how busy God gets, he still appreciates a good chuckle at the end of the day.

Sometimes, the baby even wakes my wife in the night, a moment she just has to share with me and the dog, happily spooning right next to her, dreaming our male dreams, throwing touchdowns and destroying our enemies in our sleep.

"Whaaaah?" I mumble. "What's wrong?"

"He's kicking again," she says.

"Go back to sleep," I say.

"Oh, look at that," she says.

"Ants?"

"The full moon," she says peering out the window. "It's going over the mountain."

So at 3 in the morning, my wife, the dog and I sit at the window watching the harvest moon go over the spine of a nearby mountain.

"Oh, look, look," she says as if spotting angels in the moonlight.

"OK already, I'm looking," I say.

The dog licks my ear. The baby kicks my wife's bladder. Who says a long marriage lacks intimacy? We sit there watching the moon, while being caressed and pummeled. She rubs her belly. I palm my tired eyes.

"My tummy, it's hard as a drum," she says, to which I respond, "He's all muscle, like his father," to which she responds, "But I think he's smart, too," to which I respond, "Whadaya mean by that, exactly?"

Imagine 20 years of marriage filled with conversations like this. Each day, dialogue right out of Proust.

So, this is how our nights often go lately. The days aren't quite as memorable, though last weekend we had a thrilling soccer game, in which we allowed three quick goals – Bam! Bam! Bam! – and I finally threw my pen to the ground in disgust, which was kind of embarrassing in retrospect a few days later.

I haven't thrown anything at a soccer game in three years, not since I slammed my clipboard to the ground and caught my ankle bone instead. Ouch. Still have the scar.

It's something you never forget, throwing something at a soccer game, in front of friends and foes, neither of which will ever let you live it down. In a suburb, they save such moments like baby teeth.

"I think I'm leaving," I say to my wife, after explaining the soccer fiasco.

"Finally," my wife says. "Where to?"

"Back to college," I say.

Yep, back to college. A new career. A fresh start. Back to a place where eager young minds like mine are appreciated and nurtured.

"Well, your daughter needs some bookshelves put up," my wife says. "Maybe you could visit her."

"I'm on my way," I say.

And with visions of fresh starts and frat parties, I head off again for college. A place of genuine tolerance. Cradle of the American dream.

October 2, 2002

◆ ◆ ◆

Mom, You've Got Mail

Dear Mom,

Did you know Dad was, like, coming to visit me here at college? Well, cancel the Amber Alert, he's here with his blue toolbox and a six-pack.

"Helps me work with my hands," he says as he puts the six-pack in the fridge.

Mom, what's going on? I ask him what he's doing here, and he says some men were just born to travel and explore, and he is one of them, though there isn't anything left to explore really, except our overstuffed garage, and he's kind of afraid to go in there.

He says you told him to come down here to install my bookshelves or something. Right now, he's pounding on the wall with his fist, sort of like he used to when he did our taxes.

"Hey, Dad, what are you doing?" I ask him.

"Looking for studs," he explains.

"Me, too, Daddy!" I tell him.

"Don't joke," he says and starts digging in his tool kit like some country doctor.

Can you believe this? He says that when he left home, you were lying on the couch complaining about your back and the dog was curled up next to you.

Dad said he hasn't been able to hug you in, like, two months. It's awkward to hug a pregnant woman, he says.

"You know, she quit drinking," he says.

"Dad, pregnant women usually do," I say.

"I wish someone would've warned me," he says.

Then he hands me all these letters from Columbia House that have been stacking up back home. He says he tried to warn me about Columbia House.

"It's a life sentence," he says.

"No, Daddy, it's just a record club," I tell him.

When I say this, he exhales really deep, you know, like he does instead of cursing. Big, heavy sigh. The way he did when I got that second speeding ticket.

If you ask me, I think it's freaking him out, this pregnancy. I mean, totally freaking him out.

Mom, I just can't picture Dad putting snap-crotch pajamas on some baby.

Can you? Or getting up at 2 a.m. to help with the bottle. I just can't.

Have you ever seen him try to wrap a Christmas present? Or button a dress shirt? I'm not sure he even has opposable thumbs.

"Babies are easy," he says when I bring it up.

"Um, Dad?" I say.

"Yes, sweetie?"

"Babies aren't easy," I say.

"Oh, OK," he says.

Dad says he really likes it here at college. He says the college years were the best times of his life, "if you don't count right now, of course."

"Back then, pitchers of beer were a buck," he says. "And you could get a taco for a quarter."

"Wow, Dad, you have some great memories."

"We used to have these things called toga parties," he says.

"You and Caesar?" I say.

"He was a year ahead of me," he says. "But the guy could really party."

Then he finds the wall stud and gets out his electric drill. It takes him, like, half an hour to find the drill bit thingy he needs to poke a hole in the wall.

"You know, I probably could've done this professionally," he says.

"What?"

"Hang bookshelves," he says. "I'm pretty good at it."

"I can tell," I say.

As he hangs the bookshelves, he tells me all this personal stuff, like how his AYSO soccer team lost two games in a row, and he thinks he's lost his coaching mojo.

"I've tried everything," he says. "I've switched kids around, I've added extra practices. I think I've lost my mojo."

"Maybe you should just, like, relax a little," I tell him.

"At soccer?" he says.

"It's just a game, Daddy."

"Honey, the NFL is just a game," he says. "AYSO is bigger than that."

He says the reason he's really down here is because he just needed a little break from his demanding suburban lifestyle, that's all. He might stay awhile, he's not sure. He might just hang out for a few months putting up bookshelves and teaching college kids how to shoot pool.

"By then, I'd be really good at bookshelves," he says.

Great, huh? I work all my life to get away to college, and here comes Dad with his toolbox and dopey quotations from dead people.

"Truth is just common sense clarified," he tells me at one point.

We weren't even talking about truth. He just blurts it out, all this stuff about truth.

"That's nice, Daddy," I tell him.

"Huxley said that," he says. "Thomas Huxley."

Dad says a college campus is a good place for a "binge thinker" like him, that maybe he could teach a class on soccer and hanging bookshelves and all the other things you need to know about in the real world.

"I could teach Real World 101," he says. "Believe me, I've been around."

Mom, what's he really know about the real world? He's lived in the suburbs his whole life. He coaches soccer. When I mention this, he gets all defensive.

"Honey, believe me, there's nothing more real than a suburb," he tells me. Jeesh.

He says he knows a lot of quotations I could maybe use in my term papers. Great people from throughout history. Ernie Banks. Groucho Marx.

"If you can't find a door, build one," he says.

"Um, Voltaire?"

"No, Milton Berle," he says, then starts putting his tools away.

"That's great, Daddy," I say. "Now, can you maybe fix the toilet?"

"I could probably fix toilets for a living," he says proudly.

"Good for you, Daddy," I say.

While he fixes the toilet, he starts singing. That's right, singing. Some song from Simon & Schuster. Garfunkel.

Whatever.

"And here's to you, Smokey Robinson, Jesus loves you more than you could know ... woah, woah, woah."

He says singing helps him work like this. There's not enough singing in the world, he says. Singing makes people happy.

"In college, there should be more singing," he says, then starts singing drinking songs from the 14th century.

If you ask me, I think he'll be home pretty soon.

October 9, 2002

◆ ◆ ◆

On Night Watch

IT'S 10 o'clock on a Saturday night, and we're sitting on the couch, waiting for the kids to come home.

"So where were they going after that?" I ask.

"To a party," my wife explains.

"Which party?" I ask.

We go over what the plans were after the school dance. Who was driving. Who else was in the group. It's comforting just to talk like this, to know the usual suburban surveillance system is in place, spotty as it is.

"Isn't anything else on?" I say, already struggling to stay awake.

" 'Sleepless in Seattle,' " my wife says.

"No ballgames?" I say.

"It's 10 o'clock," she reminds me.

It's been a day blessed with terrific sporting events. College football. The World Series. AYSO soccer. Is October our greatest gift or what?

Now it's 10 at night, and we're waiting for the two older kids to come home. The boy is out at a dance. The college girl is back in town and out somewhere visiting friends. On TV, Tom Hanks is reaching for Meg Ryan's hand.

"If you'd like, I could go put on my ref's uniform," I tell my wife.

"Forget it," she says.

"Too sexy?" I ask.

"Exactly," she says.

Earlier in the day, she saw me for the first time in my AYSO referee's uniform. Yellow shirt. Stretchy black shorts. Black knee socks. I looked like a human school bus. I looked like a prank.

"I'm guessing you find me kind of hot," I told her then.

"Yeah, that's it," said my wife.

It was like a male negligee, this referee's uniform. I slipped it on and suddenly she couldn't keep her eyes off me, even as she stifled a laugh. Strange what turns a pregnant woman on.

"I can't believe it," she said.

"Believe what?"

"You look like a bumblebee," she said.

"Better believe it, baby," I told her.

Tick, tick, tick.

It's 11 o'clock on a Saturday night and we're sitting on the couch, waiting for the kids to come home.

"Hey, Dad," the little girl asks. "Want to hear a song that's stuck in my head?"

"No."

"Three little pumpkins sittin' on a fence, a witch comes flying, flying by," she sings.

Even before this moment, it had been a long day. Three hours on a sunny soccer field. Like many dads, my forehead is my solar panel. It tends to hold the heat. So late on a Saturday night, I can close my eyes and feel the autumn sun in my corneas.

"Three little pumpkins sitting on a fence," the little girl sings.

"Why isn't she in bed?" I ask.

"Want some ice cream?" my wife asks.

Every time I ask a question of substance, I get answered with another question. I ask her why our youngest child isn't in bed yet. She asks me about food. Works every time.

"Want some ice cream?" my wife says again.

"Of course," I say.

As the clock ticks, I entertain my wife with gossip from the high school football game the night before. How I learned that Craig threw out his back. How Brian sold his house. How another couple had first gotten pregnant 16 years ago. You can learn a lot at a high school game, especially when the home team is behind.

"Pregnant on their wedding night?" my wife asks.

"That's what he said."

"That wasn't very good planning," she says.

My wife sits on the couch rubbing her pregnant tummy. She's eight months along and round as a Christmas ornament. Nineteen years after our first child, we're having another. How's that for planning?

"What are you going to be for Halloween?" I ask her.

"A big balloon?" asks the little girl.

"Tony Siragusa?" I say.

Neither of these ideas appeals to the pregnant wife. Women, when they blimp up like this, can be a little sensitive.

"A beach ball?" asks the little girl.

"Anna Nicole Smith?" I say.

The little girl and I finally decide that her mother should go as a shoplifter. Because she is not big and puffy the way some pregnant women get. She is big only in the tummy, as if hiding something under her shirt.

So what we're recommending is that she paint the very bottom of her tummy like a basketball, an orange crescent peeking out from beneath her maternity shirt. Like a basketball shoplifter.

"We could handcuff you too," I say.

"To whom?"

"To me," I say.

"That would be redundant," she says.

It's midnight and we're sitting on the couch, waiting for the kids to come home.

"I'm going to bed," my wife says.

"Already?" I ask.

" 'Night," she says and disappears into the shadows.

The dog, the one with the vasectomy, is sleeping next to me on the couch, snoring softly and using my bare knee as a napkin.

Slowly, my eyes begin to close. I don't know that I can hold out till the kids come home. Chances are I'll be sleeping a father's sleep – one moment snoring heavily, the next thrashing about as if making snow angels. That's how I sleep, alternately resting and exercising.

"Hi, Daddy," says the older daughter, leaning over the couch.

At first, I think it is an apparition. My lovely and patient older daughter home again. It's like a Bergman film. A moment earlier, I was worrying-dreaming about her. The next moment she is helloing me awake.

"What time is it?" I ask.

"Want some ice cream?" she asks, heading into the kitchen.

Why does the oldest kid come home first? What is the younger one up to? Can Cal beat Oregon State?

These are the questions that occupy fathers late in the night, as we sit on the couch nursing our weekend wounds.

Has the stock market finally rebounded? Can I ever retire? Where'd my wife put that leftover chicken?

On TV, Sam Malone is reaching for the barmaid's hand. Good luck, pal. She's playing you like a guitar. It's happened to men before.

And on the couch, the dog snores softly, just him and me, waiting for a kid to come home.

October 23, 2002

◆ ◆ ◆

The Pregnant Dad

SHE'S eight months pregnant, yet I'm the one who's dilated. Noticed it this morning, when I was putting on my running shoes.

"Five centimeters," I tell her.

"That's your mouth," my wife says.

"Well, technically, sure," I say.

On TV, Cary Grant is romancing Grace Kelly. I'm flipping through the channels on Saturday morning, looking for a college football game. Ohio State. Miami. Instead, I get this, a sexy woman on the make. Like I don't get enough of that in real life.

"To you, words are just play things," Cary Grant is telling Grace Kelly.

"Six centimeters," I tell my wife.

"Shhhhh," she says, turning up the TV.

Cary Grant and I have a lot in common. Time and again, we're drawn to glamorous women of dubious circumstance. Women with a healthy bosom. Nice jaw line. Credit card balances through the roof.

You know the type. The only sunlight in the room tends to fall on their delicate faces. Cabs find them on rainy days. Perfect strangers pick up their bar tabs.

They have this special aura, these women. Nice teeth. Necks like violins.

"You know as well as I know, this necklace is an imitation," Cary Grant points out.

"Well, I'm not," Grace Kelly purrs.

Meanwhile, I make out my soccer lineup on the kitchen counter. The game is in an hour. I have butterflies in the belly. A game plan swirling in my head.

Do I play Brittany at midfield? No, Brittany at forward. Do I play Marisa at forward? No, Marisa at defense.

It's playoffs, you know, and I restructure this lineup over and over. At work. In my sleep.

Amy at midfield, or Amy at goalkeeper? Kristina at goalkeeper, or Kristina at defender? Playoffs make you crazy like this.

"I think," I tell my wife, "that we'll try using four defenders this week."

"Why not eight?" she says, "why not nine?"

"Is everything a joke with you?" I ask.

"Why not 12? Why not 14?" she says.

"Because we're using four," I say.

I already have nicknames for our new defense. The Four Horsemen. The Fab Four. The Four Signs of the Apocalypse.

It's a brilliant adjustment, four. Why didn't I think of it earlier? Maybe my coaching position would be more secure.

"The parents haven't fired you yet?" my friend Paul asked the other day.

"Not yet," I said.

"I've heard talk," he said.

Yes, we've all heard the talk: "He's lost control of the players. The game has passed him by."

It's pointless, this talk. All it does is tear down what we've worked so hard to build. Such as this new four-defender formation. The Fearsome Foursome, we'll call them. Or the Four Seasons.

"One parent thinks you don't yell enough," Paul said.

"Who?"

"Your wife," he said.

"The pregnant woman?"

"She might be right," he said.

Or she could just be upset over this crib situation. For weeks, she's been asking me to put the old crib together, the one we'd stored away for the grandkids. The one we need now ourselves.

When I finally did, I found a cross-piece was missing. No big deal. I'll cut a replacement piece after the playoffs.

"You know, that baby could come any day," my older daughter warns.

"It could?"

"Dad, the due date is three weeks away."

"It is?"

"Poor Mom," she says.

What about poor Dad? The pregnant dad. I'm dilated at least 7 centimeters now. My coaching career is in disarray. My own kids don't listen to me. Only the dog will kiss me like he means it.

And, in my heart of hearts, I know that if I repair this old crib – say, this afternoon – I know that there will be a new baby in it by nightfall. In our family, an empty baby crib becomes a self-fulfilling prophecy.

All night long, there'd be a newborn in there, demanding things I can't give. Milk. Talc. Money. As Lenny Bruce once asked about babies: "Why invite a stranger into the house?"

"Maybe I should just go out and buy a new crib," Grace Kelly threatens.

Or was it my crazy-pregnant-glamorous wife, the one I can no longer wrap my arms around? The one with the movie-star glow.

These drama queens, you can hardly tell them apart anymore.

November 20, 2002

◆ ◆ ◆

The Delivery

SO the baby enters the world the way we'd all like to be – naked and skinny as a goal post – at 8:59 on a hazy Thursday morning. Profound is probably too weak a word.

Right away, two women wipe him down with gauze, as if to assure him he's come to a good place.

"He's a clean baby," a nurse says.

"We stress that," I say.

There's a little slime behind his ears, but otherwise he is indeed a clean baby, born with a clear conscience and the kind of wide-open arteries that usually come only from virtuous living and a bland diet. That'll all change quickly enough. Soon, the stain of the world will be upon him.

"We want him to cry," the nurse says.

"Show him my Visa bill," I say.

"When he cries, it gets the oxygen deep in the lungs," she explains.

"I'll tell him about the Cubs," I say.

The day began early – too early, even for two parents used to chronic sleep deprivation. We rose before the bread trucks, just as the newspaper thwacked the driveway.

"I'm already tired," I say on the way to the hospital.

"Look at that star," my wife says, pointing to the east. Seriously, the east.

"I think it's a planet," I say.

"I think it's a star," she says.

It doesn't occur to me till later the significance of two people off to have a baby, spotting a bright star in the east. Talk about historical baggage.

But what better time for a little religion, a couple in their mid-40s having yet another child, with a house already full of kids and pets and bills, sitting on the desk like a pile of leaves.

"Your Verizon account is past due," a voice on the phone had said the day before.

"We've been busy," I explained.

On the way to the hospital, the car brakes squeak. Notice how your brakes always seem to fail around the holidays? December: good for babies, bad for brakes.

"If you park on the street, you won't have to pay," my wife says, as if reading my mind.

"I'll drop you off first," I say.

In a few minutes, we are inside the hospital preparing to have another child. The other three are home, dreaming their Christmas dreams, fantasizing about all the stuff we can't afford. Snowboards. Concert tickets. College.

And here we are, having yet another one, following some strange predawn beacon to this little hospital on the hill. Does God know what he's doing? Let's hope someone does.

"Have you taken Lamaze class?" the nurse asks, going down her checklist.

"Sure," I say. "About 20 years ago."

Despite the best intentions, a dad is merely a walk-on at these events. In a maternity ward, the fathers all blend into the background. To the doctors, the dads are invisible. To the nurses, a source of amusement.

"I remember one time, I had the surgical mask on upside-down," I say. "The nurses thought it was hilarious."

"One time, we had a dad put his surgical boots over his arms," a nurse says.

What a riot we dads are. Just don't let us near the babies.

"Want to cut the cord?" a nurse is suddenly asking, bringing us back to the moment.

"Sure," I say, then snip the umbilical cord with a pair of scissors.

"He OK?" my wife asks.

"Nearly perfect," I say.

A few minutes later, the baby and I wait in the room for his mother to return from delivery. He's wrapped like a burrito. His eyes try to find focus. He's probably hoping to see a Rockefeller. Instead, he sees me.

"Your mom will be here soon," I assure him. We wait. We look at the door. We wait some more. The phone rings.

"What's he weigh?" a friend asks.

"Thirty-four pounds, 11 ounces," I say.

"That's pretty big," he says.

"I've had bigger," I say.

I hang up the phone and tell the baby about the mom he's about to meet.

The longer we wait, the more excited he gets.

"Wait'll you see her," I whisper. "She'll take your breath away."

He lifts his chin. He rolls his eyes. He yelps a little, then hiccups.

"The first time I saw your mother, wow," I tell him. With that, the baby cries. Another kid, another open mouth, another blessing.

Wow.

December 11, 2002

◆ ◆ ◆

The Index

OTHER BOOKS FROM THE LOS ANGELES TIMES

DRAWING THE LINE
by Paul Conrad
Two hundred drawings, spanning the period from the late 1960s to President Clinton's impeachment trial, from America's premier political cartoonist. $25.45

ETERNALLY YOURS
by Jack Smith
Who can forget Jack Smith, the *Los Angeles Times'* columnist for nearly 40 years? When he died in 1996, we all lost a treasure. But at least his words survived. Here, Jack's widow, Denise, and his sons, Curt and Doug, have collected some of their favorite columns. $16.95

CURBSIDE L.A.
An Offbeat Guide to the City of Angels
by Cecilia Rasmussen
Enjoy a truly eclectic tour of Los Angeles. Explore the L.A. you've not seen with enticing excursions into the city's peerless history and diversity. $19.45

DAY HIKERS' GUIDE TO SOUTHERN CALIFORNIA
by John McKinney
Walks in Southern California, from the simply scenic to the challenging, as described by *Los Angeles Times* hiking columnist and author John McKinney. $16.45

52 WEEKS IN THE CALIFORNIA GARDEN
by Robert Smaus
How to make the most of your garden by the foremost authority on gardening in Southern California. $17.45

ANSWERS FOR CALIFORNIA GARDENERS
by Robert Smaus
Expert advice in an easy-to-read Q&A format from the foremost authority on Southern California gardening. An excellent companion to Smaus' *52 Weeks in the California Garden*. $21.45

IMAGINING LOS ANGELES
Photographs of a 20th Century City
Foreword by Ray Bradbury
Collected here are some 175 photos from more than a dozen Southern California archives that tell the tale of men and women from all over the world who hoped and dared on a grand scale and who turned Los Angeles into the quintessential 20th century city. $28.95

L.A. UNCONVENTIONAL
by Cecilia Rasmussen
Where some people see roadblocks, others, such as the men and women in this volume, see possibility, opportunity and excitement. $30.95

THE SAN FERNANDO VALLEY
America's Suburb
by Kevin Roderick
Valley native Kevin Roderick recounts the area's vibrant past, from its Native American residents through the Spanish, Mexican and American settlers, spinning along the way the tales that give the Valley its unique history and culture. $26.45

LAST OF THE BEST
90 Columns from the 1990s
by Jim Murray
The best of Jim's columns from the last decade of his life are included in this paperback volume compiled by *Los Angeles Times* Sports Editor Bill Dwyre and featuring a foreword by Dodger legend Tommy Lasorda. $19.45

THE GREAT ONES
by Jim Murray
The top men and women of the sports world written about as only this late, great sports columnist could. Foreword by Arnold Palmer. $24.45

PLASCHKE
GOOD SPORTS, SPOILSPORTS, FOUL BALLS
AND ODDBALLS
by Bill Plaschke
Nearly 70 articles from the award-winning
sports columnist that will leave you laughing,
crying and wishing for more. $23.95

LOW-FAT KITCHEN
by Donna Deane
From the pages of the *Los Angeles Times* Food
section come more than 110 recipes that use
fresh food flavor, not fat, to satisfy your taste
buds. $20.45

THE LOS ANGELES TIMES' MODERN CALIFORNIA COOKING
Staff of The Times' *Food section*
A sequel to the 1981 bestseller, *California
Cookbook, Modern California Cooking* offers
more than 300 recipes that reflect the cut-
ting-edge, international cuisine for which
Southern California has become so famous in
recent years. An ideal companion to the 1981
volume. $22.45

SOS RECIPES
30 YEARS OF REQUESTS
by Rose Dosti
This bestselling hardcover book offers hundreds of tried-and-true recipes for all-time
favorite dishes that literally range from soup
to nuts. $19.45

DEAR SOS
FAVORITE RESTAURANT RECIPES
by Rose Dosti
Rose Dosti has culled her perennially popular
column in the *Los Angeles Times* Food section
to handpick 225 of all-time favorite recipes
from restaurants throughout the country.
$22.45

SUNSET BOULEVARD
CRUISING THE HEART OF LOS ANGELES
by Amy Dawes
A guide to the sights, experiences and lost
legends of Los Angeles' most famous boulevard. Loaded with photos, maps and tips on
where to dine, party and shop. $28.45

ICONIC L.A.
STORIES OF L.A.'S
MOST MEMORABLE BUILDINGS
by Gloria Koenig
The architecture and drama behind 13 of Los
Angeles' most recognizable landmarks, in-
cluding the Bradbury Building, the Getty
Museum, Disney Concert Hall and the LAX
Theme Building. With an introduction by
Frank O. Gehry. $29.95

◆ ◆ ◆

To order, call (800) 246-4042 or visit our Web
site at http://www.latimes.com/bookstore